I am curious about their verse,
The formal plots,
Rose and marble and nightingale.
This is not the poetry we know,
The hawk's lonely station
The furling, fall, unfurling,
Beauty clawed out of death.
Put me ashore at the first tavern
Among their troubadours.
I must study this rhyming.
I am anxious concerning my craft.

George Mackay Brown

Give no ground, soul.
Grasp all that ever mattered . . . ,

You did not come
With the cap of happiness,
But guardians were placed
Around your wooden cradle.

Poor guardians they were:
Iron tongs hanging over you,
A piece of your father's clothing,
Poker in the fire. . . .

Mairtin O Direain

I am just a little boy
Who's looking for a little girl
Who's looking for
A boy like me. . . .

Ira Gershwin and
George Gershwin

Bog-Trotter

Bog-Trotter

An Autobiography with Lyrics

by Dory Previn

Drawings by Joby Baker

Doubleday & Company, Inc. Garden City, New York
1980

Library of Congress Cataloging in Publication Data Previn, Dory. Bog-trotter. 1. Previn, Dory—
Biography. 2. Authors, American—20th century—Biography. I. Title. PS3566.R42Z515 818'.5'409
[B] ISBN 0-385-14708-2 *Library of Congress Catalog Card Number 78-20094 Copyright © 1980 by Dory
Previn All Rights Reserved Printed in the United States of America First Edition*

To
Alice Bach
and
Philip Mandelker

Bog-Trotter

chapter 1

... he waited
past forever
to keep his love alive
but
the girl
did not arrive.

The second song I wrote was called, "The Girl." The lyric begins by telling an ordinary story. A boy sits under the moon, smoking a cigarette, waiting for a girl. But the boy waits till he grows old. He waits till the moon gets dim. He waits till the universe disappears. The girl never arrives. The lyric was a mystery. Did he wait for someone who was real? Or was he listening for someone who didn't exist? Why did he wait at all? I was angry with myself for not being able to work it out. But the song was a riddle I wasn't to solve until my moon went dim. Till my universe damned near disappeared. I couldn't know it then, but it would be twenty-five years before I understood those simple-minded words.

Song-writing had become my avocation since I showed a four-line poem to a man. He reluctantly said I had talent. I couldn't believe it. For years I'd cursed my luck. A struggling, unsuccessful actress and tap-dancer, getting nowhere fast. First in New York, then in Chicago. Waiting for the big break by filling in as a model, chorus girl, part-time secretary. Weekends I worked as a baby-sitter. Sometimes I sang in saloons. But my voice wasn't very good. So I figured if I did special material, the audience would be caught up in the song and not notice the unspecial voice. I couldn't afford to pay a professional. And set out to write myself an act.

It was comprised of second and third choruses to all my favorite songs. Later I taught myself to write original lyrics by the same method. I imitated Cole Porter, Lorenz Hart, Oscar Hammerstein, Johnny Burke, Irving Berlin. From their work I learned construction until I could develop my own style. At that time there was no place to go to learn the craft of song-writing. Even today there are few opportunities available. When I lecture in song-writing courses, I suggest to aspiring writers they follow that example. There are no better teachers than those men.

When my act was written, I was booked in Milwaukee in a club called Fazio's. After my first show, the owner crooked his finger at me. I followed him into his office. Listen kid, he said, I'm about to save you twenty years of heartbreak. You're no good. You can't sing. You're wasting time in this business. Last month I had a singer here, Eydie Gorme. Ever hear of her? Now that's a singer. You. Forget it! One thing, though. Your material's pretty good. Who wrote it?

I left Milwaukee the next day and headed back to Chicago. My head was split between rejection and expectation. If I could write, I had to find out in a hurry. I sent some lyrics to Leonard Sillman, the producer of a series of Broadway shows called *New Faces*. He called me in Chicago and asked when I'd be in New York. In two weeks, I lied. And went out and bought a coach ticket on a train back to New York.

The weekend before I left I baby-sat for the last time. I had only forty-six dollars left and needed the extra money. While the child slept, I watched television. There was a program coming from Los Angeles. One of the featured performers was a young musician named André Previn. Two months later I was in Los Angeles, under contract to MGM Studios. Hired to collaborate on songs with the pianist-composer. I'd been writing a total of four months.

I arrived in New York and couldn't get Sillman on the phone. My forty-six dollars plus ran out. I slept on the floor of a girl friend's one-room apartment. I was desperate, with little more than the clothes on my back. Then a series of coincidences occurred. My girl friend showed my lyrics to someone who sent them to Arthur Freed, the producer of some of MGM's greatest musicals. He sent a plane ticket and a telegram telling me to come to the studio as a possible junior writer. He guaranteed me three weeks. My girl friend's friend said, You can't go out to Hollywood dressed like a beggar. He loaned me some money and I bought a new dress on the way to the airport. It took all my courage to get on that plane alone. With my luck I'd crash before I made it big. Any trip was a path to possible destruction. *They* were everywhere, Irish Catholic demons, waiting to get me. I carefully noted the initials on the side of the plane to be sure they spelled a word indicating a good omen. I went to California for three weeks and stayed twenty-five years.

Arthur Freed was kind but forgetful. He told me I would be André's lyricist but he neglected to tell him. Every time the composer passed my office I'd nervously wave a lyric at him and yell, Whenever you're ready, I am! Finally André asked, Who the hell is that weird girl with the scraps of paper? Oh, didn't I tell you? said Freed. She's your new collaborator. Well, Jesus! said André. The least you could've done was introduce us. We never wrote together at MGM. André went to France to score *Gigi*. I stayed on, writing lyric after unseen lyric. Freed was the producer of *Gigi* and was also gone. It seemed as though he'd forgotten my presence entirely. I hoped he'd return before someone higher up got wise to the fact I was there. I felt I collected a salary under false pretense. And more and more I sensed the cop at the studio gate was giving me the fish-eye. Certainly there was no welcoming nod from him as I slunk past without Freed's paternal arm about my shoulder. When André got back he would have seen my lyrics for the first time. But it was too late. My option had already been dropped.

I went to work writing songs for a cartoon company and fell in love with a married man. He told me I was irrational and should see an analyst. Which I obediently did. My confusion lay in the fact I loved him and believed he would leave his wife for me. He said he loved me but couldn't leave his older wife, his reason being his young daughter. I had a nervous breakdown.

The analyst forbade me to continue the affair. I left the sanatarium and found my job had been filled. I took part-time work as a file clerk and bookkeeper. Every day I wrote. When I had a group of satisfactory songs together I got up the guts to call André. He read the lyrics and was impressed. Our initial collaboration was called "My Heart Is a Hunter."

> . . . my heart is a hunter
> and vows to roam
> till it will find
> till it will find
> a home.

I brought the songs to a record company. The producer said, Who's that singing on the demo? Me, I said apologetically. I hadn't the money to hire someone with a good voice. Your voice is good enough for a writer, he said. Now if you can get Previn to play for you, I'll let you make an album. I was convinced André would refuse and was stunned when he agreed to accompany me.

Our first three songs written as a team were recorded in that first album, *Leprechauns Are Upon Me*. I hated the title, afraid it would give away my low-class roots. But the producer insisted, and I went along obediently so as not to make waves. I had reason to doubt my legitimacy, but it was a subject I never discussed with anyone. Not even myself.

In the beginning, André and I wrote mainly for the pleasure and experience of working together. We dreamed of our first million seller. Of some day writing a film musical. Perhaps even a Broadway show. I had a third dream. Two years later, it came true. André was scoring another film at MGM. He went to meet Freed and Vincente Minnelli on a Monday morning. Freed said to him, Well, kid, what did you do over the weekend? André replied, I got married. Oh? Anybody I know? I don't know if you remember her, said André. Her name was Dory Langdon. Of course I remember her, said Freed. Then he turned to Minnelli and said, *I* introduced them.

Just before our wedding, André scored *Porgy and Bess*. Sidney Poitier played Porgy. I assumed Porgy meant porky. As in pig. Porky Pig. That's all, folks. One night I had a bad dream. I was on my knees, my legs were paralyzed. I was Porgy. As in *pig in the parlor*. Which was another name for black Irish. *Lace curtain* meant white Irish. A higher class, they could stand up to anybody. Whereas the black Irish were shoeless beggars who ate swill and lived in the bog.

What does G stand for? I'd asked when André signed our marriage license. Nothing, he said. I wasn't given a middle name so I picked G, for George. Who's George? I asked. Nobody, he replied. As for me, I wished to God I hadn't been given a middle name. Veronica, Nica, Nick. When I was little, a kid told me Old Nick was the true name of the Devil and that scared the Bejesus out of me. Especially since my three initials, D.V.L., were closely related to the word Devil, and was it any wonder he'd dogged me ever since, me having taken his own true name while not being at all sure if my own name were false? Oh, but I'd agreed with my analyst to put thoughts like that out of my mind. For whenever a religious association reared its head it was a sign I was in danger of growing irrational.

Before we tied the knot I told André I'd had something called a nervous breakdown. I was afraid to go too deeply into details and was relieved when he seemed disinclined to go any further with the subject. In fact he avoided the subject as much as I. Questions were kept to a minimum, answers were dealt with in songs. The first lyric I dedicated to André was called "Yes." It was a youthful promise to give in to whatever he asked. Unless he asked to leave me. That was my only no. To anything else he might ever request, no matter how difficult, I would forever say, yes.

> . . . yes yes
> to every question
> yes to every whim
> i've no other answer
> when it comes
> to him.

chapter 2

The first song I wrote had the weighty title, "If Love Could Only Reason with the Moon." I was eleven. The lyric asked, Why couldn't love and the moon reason with each other? Cooperate instead of fight for love and glory. Then when arms were full, the moon would oblige by being full. I finished the lyric and tore it to pieces. Then I flushed it down the toilet. I must have hated it a lot. On the other hand, I've been known to throw away things I love.

During childhood I always seemed to be loving boys who didn't love me back. The first boy who ever *said* he loved me was named Alan Baron. We met at camp. After vacation he wrote me my first love letter. My mother got to the mailbox before me and opened it. How could she? Raised an obedient child, I swallowed my question. She smiled knowingly at the letter's gushy contents. But the thing that intrigued her was the spelling of Alan's first name. She'd only ever seen it spelled Allen. A-L-A-N was such an elegant spelling. Maybe it was English. She went on and on while I stood red-faced, scared she'd show it to my father and he'd tease me unmercifully for having a boy friend. Besides, daddy hated the English for invading Ireland.

He also carried a grudge against his own kind. We had a right to call ourselves names like bog-trotter, he used

to say, but nobody else did. He refused to connect us
with the nationality of our ancestors. All of whom had
come to this country from that green island across the
gray Atlantic just a generation before.

> leprechauns
> are upon me
> pixies are playing tricks . . .

We are Americans! he used to say. But we are of Irish
descent! Mama used to say, And proud of it! Proud of
being pig in the parlor? said Daddy. Lace curtain! said
Mama. We were never pig-in-the-parlor Irish, we were
lace curtain! Mama's father, Patrick Shannon, was very
even-tempered and had a steady job as a streetcar con-
ductor. I didn't know how Daddy could call such a
mild-mannered, dependable man black Irish. As for my
grandma Shannon, when she was a girl I know she had
shoes. She used to walk barefoot to church and carry
them under her arm so as not to wear out the soles. But
the minute she arrived she'd put them on spit-polished
like new so no one could ever accuse her of being a
bog-trotter.

Mama should have defended them to Daddy. But her
lot in life was martyrdom, his was craziness. She was
scared of him. He was scared of his own rage. I was
scared of both and would have said something except I
was a child and had no say. When I grew up I resolved
never to argue, never to raise my hand to another,
never to be beaten. I'd be a good wife, and when I had
children, my good husband would know they were his,
they would never say no to their betters. When finally

my mother handed the love letter to me I took it into the bathroom and read it several times so I would remember it always. Then I tore it up and down the drain it went.

chapter 3

Every Saturday afternoon my father took me on the bus to Perth Amboy for tap-dancing lessons. Not toe dancing — that meant leaps, twirls, flying. And I was a grounded being. But I envied those marvelous flyers, acrobats, tumblers, ballerinas. The ballet teacher was my angel-ideal, though she was never my teacher. A beautiful, slender woman with long legs and straight hair. One afternoon the angel graced the tap class with a live performance. She spun like a globe. Balanced on the delicate point of a toe. Leapt like a spirit. Hung suspended by invisible cords. And concluded with an aerial split. By some pure, high, heavenly means, she was able to dance on air.

Leaving the studio that Saturday, I came upon her slippers on the floor of the changing room. The curve of one divine toe was turned inward under the heel of the other. Next to the still crisscrossed ribbons lay a wad of used lamb's wool. I picked it up and stuffed it into my sweater pocket. When I got home I hid under the front stoop and examined my prize. Was it made of separate strands or one long endless thread? I tried to untangle the knots, but it refused to unravel. The harder I pulled, the tighter it got. Never would I learn the secret. What made her fly? I smelled the wool and felt embarrassed at the animal odor. My angel sweats just like me? Well, if she smelled the way I smell, she couldn't be so terrific. I was so disappointed in her I bit the wool and threw it away.

Then I began to miss my souvenir, thread to the stars. Perhaps I'd mistaken the odor. It must have been from my own hands. Wasn't Mama always saying to me, Dorothy, take your paws off yourself! I was the dirty monster. An angel on high would not offend. I went back to retrieve the lamb's wool. It was gone. Rain must have washed it out from under the porch. It could have been carried away by any one of the network of muddy rivulets that patterned our unpaved road.

chapter 4

> my daddy say
> i ain't his child
> ain't that somethin'
> ain't that wild . . .

Very early in my life, I heard something that left a constant underlying uncertainty about my identity. My mother told my Aunt Rose that my father said I wasn't his child. As I grew older, I constantly experimented with variations on my name, but insecurity kept me from straying too far from the original. My mother named me Dorothy. My father named me Langan. School friends called me Dot.

I left home to be an actress. I wound up being a chorus girl. I wanted to be more snappy. I became Dottie Langan. Nobody could pronounce Langan. A simple enough name, yet people always asked me if it were Lannigan or Langton or Langdon. I decided to become Dottie Langdon. I aspired to become a model. Dottie, the ex-chorus girl, sounded dumb. I thought I achieved an aura of elegance by returning to Dorothy Langdon. It sounded a bit English. The Anglican affectation was fine for the part-time model, temporary baby-sitter. But when Dorothy began to seriously write, another change was in order. More intelligent, artistic. Something with an accent. Doré. It sounded poetic. Doré Langdon, the lyricist, forced herself onto the plane for Hollywood where the head of the studio turned out to have picked the same damned name, without the accent. Before Doré checked into MGM Studios she decided the spelling was too French. Dorrie was too close to the chorus girl. Dot was too Irish and Dorothy was as old-fashioned as tap dancing. But Dory was just right. It rhymed with story. And Dory was a writer. She had a three-week contract as proof.

chapter 5

A marriage contract did little to quell the old sense of illegitimacy. The questionable identity refused to stay buried under the weight of all those names and disguises. It seemed to me that people were unable to remember *any* of my names. Dory who? Oh yes, André's wife. No one recognized me, I imagined, except as Mrs. Previn. So after three years of marriage, I chose to change my name again. I began to write under Andre's name. Previn as a label opened doors and charge accounts, slightly lessened the feeling of intimidation by headwaiters, and got me past the cop at the studio gate. When we were divorced, identity inevitably arose. Not my father's child. Not my husband's wife. There was no going back to Langan or Lannigan or Langdon. And if I lost Previn, who the hell would I be? So I kept André's name. I kept it and *used* it.

You could say I also used my father's name since he was obstinately reluctant to take responsibility for my presence. The one person whose name I had a right to was my mother. I came screaming from her womb. She never let me forget it. Thirty-three hours! she used to say. Thirty-three long hours of labor I pushed with you! But you didn't seem to care if you ever came out and why should you come out to a father who'd make it clear you were not wanted? The Langans are terrible-tempered, the Devil's in him, that's the truth!

Shannon, her maiden name, was a river in Ireland. No longer do I feel a need to ride on another person's identity. Today I tread water cautiously close to the moss-bound bank of that river, sure of only one thing, I am my mother's child. It may be a wise child who recognizes its father, but it's a backward child who recognizes its mother. Back I went, stupidly pursuing a reflection in the subconscious stream that winds through the lower marsh. When first I heard the reflection whisper, Dory of Shannon, I fled in fear from the greeting. In all directions. It took years to return that small hello. Before that, running from bottom to top, there were divorce, separation, insanity, career, and marriage.

Marriage to a well-known composer would open the high world to me. The tap dancer from New Jersey still had problems getting off the ground. But a peasant wife is able to squat in the shadow of her glorious lord. He spoke three languages. It was thrilling to be distantly related to those beautiful creatures who fly.

> . . . the world is my palace
> i feel just like alice
> when she stepped
> into the mirror!

You made me love you
I didn't want to do it
I didn't want to do it
You made me want you
And all the time you knew it
I guess you always knew it
You made me happy sometimes . . .

> *J. V. Monaco and J. McCarthy*
> *(letter from Judy Garland to Clark Gable)*

chapter 6

On the far side of the continent I'd watched Judy Garland on the screen of the local movie house and wanted to be her. The memory was still vivid of when she wrote that letter to her hero in Hollywood, Clark Gable. Now, for a film called *Pepe*, I'd written "The Faraway Part of Town" for her. It was like one of the plots of her movies.

A decision came down from the top. She shouldn't appear. Someone thought she was too overweight. I didn't think so. I'd have taken her under any conditions. At our first meeting she was in radiant spirits. She had us in stitches with stories of the great days at MGM. She wickedly mimicked prissy leading ladies and rough, tough heroes. As for the not-so-great days, she struck back with the same humor. The most awful story had a hilarious punch line. She dealt with adversity by laughing her head off. André and I played several songs for her. She liked them all. Later, she recorded "Yes." I was deeply grateful for her generosity.

Many singers resent the fact they don't write the words they're interpreting. She had admiration and respect for the writer. To me she seemed to be so secure in her own talent, she would never need to waste time resenting that of others. In *Pepe* her sound soared gloriously over the trivial action on the screen. In my opinion, she was never in better voice. Thanks to her, I had my first Academy Award nomination, together with André. We were on our way. Nothing could go wrong.

We went to the Academy Awards ceremonies. The crowds frightened me. I attributed it to expectation. We didn't have a chance of winning. Even so, a part of you prepares for the impossible. In the back of your head is the vague form of an acceptance speech. Whom would I thank? When I told my father I was going to Hollywood he said, To do what? I said, To be a writer. A writer? he said. So you couldn't make it as an actress! And my mother said, I hope you don't get hurt. When I realized I hadn't won an Oscar, I wanted to get up and yell, Oh shit! And stomp out of the theater. To this day, when I see those losers stiffly smiling for their public and for the TV camera, I long for one brave soul to show us what we know he's really feeling.

> control yourself
> contain yourself
> restrict yourself
> restrain yourself
> and always let
> tranquility
> be your goal . . .

you must
contain yourself
restrain yourself
and train yourself
to gain your
self control!

chapter 7

My ambition was to write lyrics which enhanced the characters and story in a film. I hated *title* songs that were thrown in over the end credits for no purpose other than exploitation. I was determined to develop my own style of dramatic writing. Literate, yet popular. A combination of French chanson and Country Western. An advanced and hopeless aspiration in those days, the late fifties and early sixties, before Dylan and the Beatles came on the scene. The second Academy nomination André and I had was for a song called "Second Chance."

The assignment was a lyric for the theme of *Two for the Seesaw*. The leading character, Gittel Mosca, played by Shirley MacLaine, was touching and tough. I chose to pattern my song on Gittel. Walter Mirisch, the producer, met us on the sound stage and I sang the song for him. When we finished, Mirisch said it wouldn't do. Why not? we asked. Because it gives away the ending, he said. People will hear it on the radio and they won't go to see the movie. Reluctantly, I made changes. Regardless of the rejection, I took the criticism as a compliment. If I could write a whole damned movie in about twenty lines, I figured I did a good, economical job of story telling.

It's odd how a style changes into its own opposite. Many years later United Artists engaged me to write a lyric for Gato Barbieri's theme of *Last Tango in Paris*. I never met the director, Bernardo Bertolucci, but I watched the film many times and thought I had an inkling of his subtext. They key was in his use of mirrors reflecting an empty room reflected through a camera lens to be projected onto a screen. The two strangers came together as prisms in cracked crystal, several times removed from reality. They were shadows who dance. I borrowed his images and felt his intention was served. The publisher, Murray Deutsch, thought differently. He objected to the shadows and mirrors and reflections. He said the images were not masculine. Not masculine? I asked. According to *who*? According to him. I held off an attack of tears with a cliché question. If I were a man, would he feel the same way about the images? He felt no need to reply. With false bravery, I said he didn't have to pay me, we could forget the contract. He stunned me by accepting the offer. Then I heard he was looking for a male lyricist.

Meanwhile, someone who liked the lyric read it to Bertolucci. He was pleased that it told his story. Word was sent back the director liked the lyric; my *deal* was suddenly on again. Deutsch and I were never able to reconcile our differences of opinion. Eventually, he admitted all my lyrics embarrassed him. I noticed in my printed copies, some *undesirable* lines had actually been censored and rewritten. We parted company. There's an interesting coda to the story. The melody of the song, as often happens with a scoring theme, was dramatically rangy, too difficult for most pop singers. Andy Williams made a fine version, as did Marlena Shaw. Neither the male nor the female record made it. Why not?

I think the reason is that my lyric was wrong. The man and woman in the film weren't shadows who dance. They were people who ran. As soon as they split from that room they were doomed. A life alternative would be to stay in that confined space and play and replay their relationship till all the layers were stripped away. Till both sides were ruthlessly told and all secrets were heard. Till no illusions were left and all shadows were lit. When they stopped grasping at each other they might have begun to grasp *their selves*. Making possible a path towards the birth of true reflection instead of destruction and death.

> don't you know
> that the blood
> in your vein
> is as lifeless
> as yesterday's rain?
> it's a game
> where we come
> to conceal
> the confusion we feel
> long as we're nameless
> our bodies are blameless . . .

For the second time I lost an Oscar. Meanwhile André won two. One was for *Porgy and Bess*. There were other dreams like the first Porgy dream. One night I dreamed I was legless and armless. On a chessboard. I was a rook trying to keep in the game on the nearly empty board. I stayed absolutely still for a long time. Then I made my move into the next square by bending face down and pulling my limbless torso by my forehead. I should have paid closer attention to my identification with Porgy. And with his name. But in those days I didn't track everything down for fear of what I'd find. Then too I couldn't admit not even to myself that I was a bog-trotter. A shoeless hunter of clues in the bleak past, a pursuer of the mouth of the spring in the swampland of origins. Porgy was trying to tell me things. Things I wasn't prepared to hear. Today I know Porgy means a fish. Which swims in the ocean. Or in a river. Such as the river Shannon. I also know that the Irish word pota and poite are related. When such clues did rise I took a pill to dull my associations rather than let my head go deeper into the Hibernian bog. But had I pursued those mysterious connectives, I might have understood why years later I boarded a London-bound plane expecting to find Sidney Poitier in the seat next to mine. And why, when he didn't show up, my tenuous sick grasp on reality was lost forever.

> mister whisper's
> here again
> mister whisper's
> here again . . .

chapter 8

One day a phone call came from a man who introduced himself as Bobby Lewis. He told André he had an idea for a musical. Could we meet with him and talk it over? André agreed and I suggested we have lunch at our house. Robert Lewis was well known to us as a very successful Broadway director. We looked forward to meeting him and hearing his idea. I prepared a terrific lunch. Omelets, home-made biscuits, salad with a very good white wine. I hoped he'd be impressed.

At the very start of the meeting we realized the man was a different Robert Lewis. He was a rehearsal pianist. André asked if he could see me for a moment. We went into the kitchen and broke out laughing. What we have here is the wrong Robert Lewis! We decided there was nothing to do but get through the lunch as well as we could without giving away our mistake.

A few months later, we told that story to Gower Champion. He laughed loudly. Then, there was a long pause. Well? said Gower. Was his idea any good? We both were stunned. We'd never taken the trouble to find out. I won't speak for André, but I now realize I was a horse's ass. Gower is shrewd, an admirable trait. He doesn't care who the person is, only about the idea.

Gower had agreed to direct a film musical version of
Goodbye, Mr. Chips. The idea was André's and mine;
another dream was about to come true. Great stars were
mentioned for the picture, including Rex Harrison and
Petula Clark. Terence Rattigan would write the screen-
play. Everyone associated with the project was a name.
What's known as above the title. All but one. A mutt
had wandered into the dog show and was pissing all
over the pedigrees. Everybody began to loathe my
lyrics.

> should i call you mister?
> should i call you sir?
> should i be a sister?
> which would you prefer?

The style for the woman was considered appropriately
feminine. Properly polite. It was the content of the male
lyrics which seemed to rankle. The leading man
couldn't be asked to admit to an unwritten book. Certainly not to fears unfought. When Katherine dies,
Chips would behave intelligently. A stable man doesn't
sing in an empty room of the loss of an unborn child.

> a star
> with a fixed expression
> calmly stares at strife
> its look is brief
> upon our grief
> empty is my life . . . .

More controlled lyric statements were in order for stars
with fixed expressions. I was removed from my own
project. André was also canceled. Judged inept by asso-

ciation? Leslie Bricusse replaced us. When we left, Gower left too. I considered André a winner. Desperately, I hoped he didn't attribute his first major loss to being with me. I didn't dare ask him, however. A possibility like that could never be questioned for fear it might uncover a truth.

Ultimately, I would get to write with many of the great scorers and composers, including Harold Arlen, Johnny Green, David Raksin, and John Williams. But, at the start, André had trouble bringing me into projects and I felt the discrimination from all sides. Then men had no hesitation about expressing prejudice against a writer because she was a female. Vernon Duke smiled indulgently when André said I was first rate. There's no such thing, said Duke, as a first-rate woman lyricist. What about Dorothy Fields? She is the one exception, said Duke. And Dory is the second, said André. Duke did a mock bow. Well, he said, I would be delighted to be proved wrong.

chapter 9

A few years ago, on a TV interview in London, John Lennon was asked if he had any favorite movie theme-songs. He mentioned one of ours. The theme of *Goodbye, Charlie.* He told a story about the Beatles singing it in India on the banks of the Ganges. The incongruity of that picture tickles me. The glorious spiritual rhythms of that timeless river accompanying a modern jazz waltz with a slangy, irreverent lyric.

There was another on that trip. A young girl named Mia Farrow. Though I wasn't to meet her till later. Karma has an elfin sense of humor. It makes its presence known in the most ridiculous patterns. Nothing seems to match, yet everything matches. The river winds, the thread unravels, moments pass in three-quarter time. A symbol of the eternal triangle. With such *irrelevant* words.

> there ain't no doubt
> strike three
> you're out
> goodbye Charlie
> goodbye . . .

The same young girl, now grown to young woman-hood, with lots of children to prove the growth, recently referred to one of my songs in print. She called "Beware of Young Girls" tasteless. I was indignant she chose to discuss me, and disappointed she hadn't said more. The critique was included in a long myth of how and when she had *really* met her then husband. Myths don't bother me, we all make up things, blarney is the nature of imagination. But, tasteless? She goes too far. Doesn't she? Let's examine the origins of the word. Taste is related to tact, tax, touch, and tango. The melody which I originally took from "The Whiffenpoof Song" is old-fashioned as a tango tune. So I can't go along with her on that. I admit it was tactless and out of touch. I wrote it at a time when I was rather out of touch. Tax means, to touch hard. The lyric did hit home, especially mine. Tax further means, to evaluate. She rates the song as without value? Yes, I suppose it is. God knows, I've not made a dime from it. But tax also means, to blame. Now she says the song is blameless. Ah well, if she means the song is tactless, out-of-touch, untaxing, valueless, and blameless, then I agree with her. It *is* tasteless.

chapter 10

Inside Daisy Clover was one of our most exciting assignments. It gave us a chance to write a musical score in the style of the thirties. Not only that, there was a place for a *big* song. The kind sung by the aspiring newcomer. Full of passion and determination. Natalie Wood played the waif who became a star. And we wrote "You're Gonna Hear from Me" for her audition scene.

It must have conveyed a sense of youth yearning to spread wings and reach for the stars. A Broadway producer told us later so many young singers used it to audition he couldn't stand to hear it one more time. Finally, in self-defense, he said he had to ban it. I was delighted. As a young tap dancer I had auditioned for the Rockettes at Radio City Music Hall. I winked, twinkled, triple-tapped and wasn't picked. But, I would eventually make that line. When *Daisy Clover* opened in New York the entire chorus of Rockettes hoofed to "You're Gonna Hear from Me." The corps de ballet soared to another song.

> everyone tells me
> to know my place
> but that ain't the way
> i play
> why am i daring
> to show my face?
> 'cause i've got
> something
> to say!

At seventeen I had gotten to tap in the chorus of a Broadway road show. One of the dancers was another teen-ager named Herbert Ross. Before we left on tour he invited me for cheese, wine, and candlelight in a one-room basement apartment. The wine was cheap and the candles were Whelan's Drug Store. But, I didn't care. It was my first encounter with romantic atmosphere. Added to that was another new experience, he read poetry to me out loud. I couldn't believe the beauty of it. I immediately fell in love. Herbert never considered me more than an acquaintance.

But that evening left an indelible impression. Outside of a few plays in acting classes, I'd read next to nothing. Whatever desire I'd had to read had been discouraged when I brought home from the library two books which my father leafed through, judged to be obscene, and burned in the furnace. I flunked in high school, couldn't afford to go to college. From a lower-class, rigidly religious existence, I'd been thrust into the world without education or preparation. On the tour I went out with lots of men. All strangers, which is the nature of travel. By the time we got to California I was pregnant and didn't know it. I left the show in Hollywood to break into the movies and instead I got an abortion.

> it disappeared
> in the red-tinted water
> i never knew
> was it a son
> or a daughter?

A bartender named Arthur Barrett let me move in with him. Despite the fact I was pregnant with somebody else's child, he loved me. And he managed to scrape the money together to pay for the abortion. I was grateful to him and deeply relieved it was over. But there were complications. Physically and emotionally. My passionless initiation into sex had brought me nothing but pain and worse, an unnatural dread of getting pregnant again. My inbred Catholicism made me see myself as a bum living in sin. A growing web of lies was stifling me with false addresses to my parents and phony names to the hotel landlord. I had to get out. In desperation I wrote my mother. She sent me the money for a bus ticket back to New Jersey. I arrived home anemic and fifteen pounds underweight.

In a short time my mother fattened me up to my normal weight. My father pressed me to get on with my *career*. Every day I took the train to New York to look for work.

Finally, I got a job as a chorus girl in a club on Eighth Avenue. The club closed. But then I made the big time. The line at the Latin Quarter on Broadway. Quickly I realized I was out of my league. With my pug-Irish features and my stumpy legs, I *missed*. Whenever a new girl was hired she was given my place and I was shifted closer to the edge of the line. Just when I reached the tail-end of the tiller, a telegram arrived from a Hollywood studio, offering me a contract. A letter with instructions would follow. I think Lou Walters, the Latin Quarter owner, accepted my two weeks' notice with relief. It saved him from the unpleasant task of firing me.

But he had a protective attitude toward his girls and he read the telegram with suspicion. He'd never heard of that particular studio, he said. But I didn't want to know about doubts. As I left his office I brushed away the impression that he was sitting there sadly shaking his head. On the other hand, the girls viewed me with new admiration. Even respect. Somehow the runt at the end of the line had achieved the dream. The letter arrived with a plane ticket. I would be met at the airport by a studio representative. Mama said a rosary for me. Daddy gave me ten dollars and a warning to watch my soul. I went to Mass and on my knees begged God not to let me crash. And I got on the plane for Los Angeles. On disembarking, I heard my name and turned. The representative was Arthur Barrett.

He'd done it, he said, to get me to come back. There was no contract. Lou Walters' suspicions had been accurate. There was no studio. The only work I could get in Hollywood was as a checkroom girl. The salary was less than adequate. But I was determined to save enough money for a ticket back home. Every night I left work limping. The hatcheck concessionaires thought it was from standing for such long hours. Actually, it was caused by the cramping of the coins. I wore shoes two sizes too big so I could steal tips.

Arthur tried to make contacts for me. Anybody who came into the bar for a drink and remotely discussed the movies was questioned about connections. He knew I was counting the tips till I could get out. Yet he valiantly strove to keep me with him. His attempts brought a few interviews and no success. In Hollywood, as later in New York, show business seemed forever closed to a tap dancer in the rise of ballet, a folk singer in the era of big bands, a guitar picker in the time of jazz, a kinky-headed girl gone bad in a world that revered straight hair and June Allyson. I was out of step with the times. A square. Yet, too experienced. Excluded from papal endorsement.

Again, I tearfully left Arthur and relievedly went back to New York by bus. After pounding the pavements without results, there was no choice but to take a job in the checkroom of the Copacabana after being turned down twice for a place in the line. It was humiliating. Whenever the Latin Quarter girls came in I tried to turn my face away or duck behind a fur stole. One girl eventually spotted me. But instead of putting me down for not making it in Hollywood, she berated me for snubbing her. I was too tongue-tied to express my feelings to her then. But I never forgot her kindness. Years later I wrote a television movie called *The Third Girl from the*

Left. It was based partly on her. And on all the other nameless girls who are identified only by the numbers assigned to them in the chorus line. Where each pair of legs is given a mark. And told to stay in its *place*.

There were other odd jobs. I got out my guitar and worked up a few folksongs in order to enter amateur contests. I was an Arthur Godfrey loser. Also a receptionist, typist, underwear model, part-time machine operator, Queen of the New Jersey State Fair and Miss Halvah. A man asked me to marry him. Rather, I asked him, since he was the only show-business Catholic I knew. With one religious gesture, I could placate my anxious parents and free myself from living in sin. During our eight-month marriage we shared my one-room apartment and a budget of a dollar a day for food. I cooked on an electric stove in the closet and regularly set my clothes on fire. Holy Matrimony didn't revive the desired evangelical fervor I sought. Neither did it have any long-range spiritual effect on my husband, apparently. After producing two flop plays he left the country and a pile of unpaid bills. Long after I perjured myself to get an annulment I read a lead article about him in *Variety*. It said he was wanted by the European police. Because he had swindled Spain.

Later, I learned there were other, darker reasons why I proposed to that particular man. When we first started seeing each other we went away for a weekend at a friend's home. We were given separate rooms. He slept on the floor above me. In the attic. During the night, despite my fear of being discovered, I felt an urgent need. I *had* to climb those stairs. To be with him. Overcoming my timidity, I sneaked up to his bed. And had the first orgasm of my life. The next day I begged him to marry me. I never had a second orgasm with him. And couldn't understand why he had so deeply affected me that one and only time. In somebody else's attic.

> with my daddy
> in the attic
> that is where my being
> wants to bed
> with the mattress ticking showing
> and the tattered pillow slip
> and the pine
> unpainted rafters
> overhead . . .

The annulment left me without legal ties in the eyes of justice. But the Church and my parents never forgave me. What does it profit a man, Daddy always asked, if he gains the whole world and suffers the loss of his soul? My mother had a mild heart attack, my sister said if she died it would be my fault. And she intended to pray every day that I would find my way back to her God. All that because I was annulled. What would they say if they knew about the abortions? There'd already been a second. I tried to put them out of my head and couldn't. Mama used to accuse me of being scared of my own shadow. But everything began to scare me, *nothing* began to scare me. I longed to be forgiven the burden of my sins and couldn't face a priest. I grew apprehensive about coming out of my rooming house, for fear I'd get hit by a car and die while still evicted from the state of grace. If only I could make my way back to my parents and God by becoming a star. Major stars were granted special dispensations by the Church. Tyrone Power was divorced. And through a special dispensation, he was married to Linda Christian with a high mass by a bishop in a cathedral.

Nights, I worried about the atom bomb. What if they dropped it on New York before I got my big break? Days were spent in the Hotel Astor ladies' room anxiously scanning the Actors' Audition Sheet. One afternoon, I went to try out for a bus-and-truck production of *Liliom*. They dismissed me as a wrong type. I met an elderly actor. We went for coffee. He listened to my complaints. I had no pull. My father said so. And he was right. There I was, not even lucky enough to get a bit part in some broken-down play nobody'd ever heard of. The actor was surprised I'd never read Molnar. He lovingly described the carnival barker and Julie, the country girl. Oh, you've made a mistake, I countered. You're talking about *Carousel*. You stupid idiot! he shouted. How dare you enter the theater with a head crammed full of popcorn! God gave you a brain, use it! How? I whined. Read! he said. Books are free! The next day I went to the public library and began at letter A.

I joined a play-reading group. There I met a young shipping clerk, Robert Schneideman. The first person I ever met with a bona-fide genius I.Q. He was my first teacher. He encouraged me to try to write. When he left New York to get his master's degree I followed him to Chicago, I recognized education as the door to survival, and he held the key. Eventually I found the courage to show him a poem. There were only four lines. Too

timid to try anything more ambitious, I had no idea
what the lines meant.

> do not ghosts belong in long vast places
> to whistle and whine and haunt the spaces
> to finger the flaws and trace the traces
> of masculine tweeds and feminine laces . . . .

His face grew strange. My God, he said. Is it possible,
you might turn into a writer? A *writer*? Don't be silly. I
had no notion of punctuation, parsing a sentence was a
mystery to me. But why not? Maybe my luck was
changing. The gift Robert gave me became the tool
through which I left him. I wouldn't presume to attempt to be a poet. My mind couldn't even comprehend
those four lines. Poetry meant using big words and I
was a terrible speller. To be taken seriously, you
needed bachelor's degrees and master's degrees, all
those male initials behind your name. But lyric writing
was not an impossibility. A woman such as Dorothy
Fields commanded respect and was considered by
some to be as good a lyricist as any man. And we
shared the same first name, maybe it was a good omen.

Now I'd returned to Hollywood as a writer. A new person. A second chance. The years in the library had
shaped my taste. I was well informed on theater, paint-
ing, and poetry. Under Robert's guidance I'd managed
to scrounge a crash-course equivalent of a college education. The bog-trotter had come up in the world. There
were setbacks. I'd grown completely dependent on my
analyst. With good reason. I dreaded all meetings with
film people. And had to fortify myself with heavier

tranquilizers than usual to appear as calmly professional as my peers. During one such occasion, I had
come from a sanitarium on a three-hour pass. No one
suspected that when the meeting ended I checked back
into the crazy-bin.

When we discussed a choreographer for *Daisy Clover*, I
excitedly proposed Herbert Ross. During the years he
had grown into a brilliant ballet choreographer. I was
always aware of his progress. Frankly, I wanted him to
be aware of mine. He was contacted and flown to
California. I planned not to mention anything to him
for a while, I wanted to keep my secret to myself so I
could savor it. At our first meeting he asked if we'd
ever met before, and I blurted out the whole story like a
schoolgirl. Herbert went on to great success as a film
director. His first directorial assignment was *Goodbye,
Mr. Chips*. When Leslie Bricusse replaced André and
me, Herbert replaced Gower Champion.

> new rooms new rooms
> i hate new rooms
> i never know
> just where to look
> i go to a shelf
> get hold of myself
> and pretend to read
> a boring book
> as though my life
> depends on it . . .

chapter 11

i watch the game
aware of tricks
i do not want to see . . .

Rejection, disappointments were part of the game, I rationalized. I had the husband I wanted and the work I loved. The two would pull me through. Meanwhile, there were pills to keep me going, only till I wouldn't need them. I'd use them, I told my analyst, I'd never let pills use me. Against the odds, I'd made a success of my life. They could never do me in completely. The small amount of acting experience was a help. I appeared to be a good woman, good lyricist, the well-adjusted good wife of a good man. I'd mocked it up that way, and was determined to conform to the dream if it killed me. There were more periods euphemistically referred to as breakdowns. Eventually, it was called by its rightful name. André described the scene to me.

Admittance papers carelessly left on the top of a desk. The husband picks them up and reads. Next to *Diagnosis Of Patient* is a blank. The space is filled in with one typewritten word: Schizophrenia. The letters leap at him from the page, like an extreme close-shot in a movie. His feeble defense against the shock is to hear it underscored. I think he said, he would have used strings and a drum.

. . . but there were times, dear,
you made me feel so bad.

(Judy Garland)

Frankly, my dear, I don't give
a damn.

(Clark Gable)

chapter 12

My last encounter with Judy Garland was very different
from the first. We were writing the songs for Mark Rob-
son's production of *Valley of the Dolls.* Judy had the featured role of a fading star. We were to meet with her at
Twentieth Century-Fox studios. She was hours late.
She arrived looking ill and insecure, thin as a bird. She
came alone. We played some songs for her. Nothing
pleased her. It's not good enough, she kept saying over
and over. It's not good enough. I think I understand
what was going on inside her, having once again
recently come out of a mental hospital. But never would
I discuss my own illness, that was the secret of the crazy
sister. The one who heard voices. Every so often, the
crazy sister had to be locked in the tower till she came
to her senses and was made to understand she didn't
hear voices. Then she could be allowed out with the
normals on one condition. That she *never* mention her
voices in front of the good woman or her good husband. She must deny that at all cost. The minute she
started talking about it, she would be indicating a

regression and would be thrown in the slammer again. I longed to tell Judy of my own problems. Maybe if, in those days, we had been able to openly discuss and share, people such as Judy would be alive. Wounds fester if they aren't opened and cleaned out. Judy Garland was the victim of a Band-Aid society. She was permitted to act it out, never to air it out.

We met again and played another song for her called "I'll Plant My Own Tree." I'll do it! she said excitedly. We were relieved. A few days later we had a call. Judy wanted to meet us at her old home studio, MGM. We got together on a sound stage. I fantasized it was one she'd worked on. Had she sung to Clark Gable there? Roger Edens arrived. He had written or arranged some of her biggest hits. We gave the song to Roger. He went over it. What do you think? Judy asked anxiously. Roger said, I think you should do it. It's perfect for you. She smiled like a happy child. Perhaps she needed to have a reassuring voice from her past validate the song. All right, she said. Now, I'll *really* do it!

I wish the story had a good ending. Judy recorded it for the sound track. She did endless takes. The final tape had eighteen splices. All the mistakes were cut out, the breaks in the voice erased. The track had been altered to appear straight, but the uneven sound only emphasized the confusion so carefully edited. There were too many splices in too short a song. When her first day of shooting arrived she was unable to come out of her dressing room. People were angry with her. I knew that feeling of not being able to come out of your room. I wasn't angry with her. I was jealous.

> when did i stop
> feeling sure
> feeling safe
> and start wondering why
> wondering why
> is this a dream
> am i here
> where are you
> what's in back of the sky . . .?

The lyric of the theme of *Valley of the Dolls* was the first time I made professional use of my own experience with drugs. The story about women on pills was right for it. I knew what pills did to the speech pattern. The way one repeats phrases and never gets out the entire sentence. I told André I wanted to write a repetitive lyric and he wrote an amazingly circular melody. Maybe he understood from a familiarity with my confusion when I was on too many pills, I don't know. Of course it was never discussed. I was fearful someone else would catch what I'd done in that lyric and the crazy sister would be given away. But no one ever mentioned it to me until a year or so later, when I was back in the hospital. That song you wrote, said a patient. Is that about somebody on reds? No, I said. Yellows.

We handed in the finished theme. Everybody liked it except Jacqueline Susann. I didn't know she had wanted to write the lyric. She wrote a second version. As the original author, she had every right. It was recorded and released. I don't know if there have ever been two simultaneous title theme songs. I don't recall who sang her version. I do recall who sang ours.

Lionel Newman, head of Fox music department, asked
who we'd like to have for the sound track. We mentioned a fine though little-known singer. Lionel shook
his head. You don't ask for her, he said. You settle for
her. Now, if you two could have anybody in the entire
world, who would it be? In the entire world? Okay,
Dionne Warwick. Dionne was then the hottest singer
around. She was sent the song. And she agreed to do it.
We were overjoyed. Her record came out too late to be
noticed at Academy voting time and wasn't nominated.
But by the time the awards were given, it had reached
number one on the *Cash Box* charts. We had our first
million seller. We were now an established team. I was
increasingly fearful of travel. That eclipsed the dream of
the Broadway musical. I wasn't holding André back.
With my encouragement he was moving away from
studio scoring toward symphony conducting. Actually
I gave him my full support for fear I'd lose him. Still, as
far as film work was concerned, there were plenty of
reasons to expect our collaboration would continue to
grow. That was the last film song André and I wrote together.

> gotta get off
> gonna get
> have to get off
> from this ride
> gotta get hold
> gonna get
> need to get hold
> of my pride . . .

They *asked me*
How I knew
My true love
Was true
I of course replied
Something here inside
Cannot be denied
They *said . . . .*

Oscar Hammerstein

chapter 13

Everyone I love, loves you. Everyone I love, loves you *both*. So I must introduce myself to you, she exclaimed. She had come all the way across Hope and Alan Pakula's patio just to meet us. The natural surroundings conspired to enhance the luminous youth. The background was lit by banks of white daisies. Delicate hands clung to a square of tapestry. She'd been stitching an old rose pattern. The sun danced attendance on the point of the needle and silken straight thread of her hair. The skin was translucent, as though she were still wrapped in the gauze of her placenta. The voice had been gently buffed by good schools and privilege. She would never need to raise her tone to get something she wanted. She came of a film-director father and a movie-star mother. No pig in the parlor, she. This was lace-curtain Hollywood. She was second-generation MGM. And the newly famed waif wanted to be our friend. I was more than eager to comply. André seemed less impressed.

> it's not that you're different
> you're just as you were
> why you're even wearing
> the tie i prefer
> it's nothing that shows
> yet the certainty grows
> you've had
> a change of heart.

One night we drove to a restaurant with her and Mike Nichols. She announced to Mike she was the only one to play Peter Pan. For in fact, she'd been to Never-Never-Land many, many times. You've been to no such place, Mia! said my husband. If you ever say anything so stupid again, I'll personally throw you out of the car! I wondered why she always annoyed him. And I was secretly glad. It had become difficult for a woman, forty and more, to see a girl, much less than twenty and four, in any guise other than perfect. And that perfection was beginning to threaten. I tried to remember other times when André might have seen her at a disadvantage. There was the night she'd had too much to drink at the Bricusses' and we had to drive her home. Then there was Adolph and Phyllis Green's party when everyone was dancing to rock. I was too embarrassed to try. New steps had replaced the old. The ex-tap dancer was ill at ease with the relentless beat. I covered my obsolescence with disdain. But it cut deeper than that. The media-oracles of pop music had deemed the lyric passé. And if words went completely down the drain, what would be left for me?

She drifted onto the floor. I clearly recall everything she wore. A tam with a pom-pom, a knitted scarf, and *knee socks*. Oh Christ, I thought, if only I could be young enough once more to wear knee socks. My self-esteem got a sudden jolt. I was delighted to see that on the dance floor, beauty is not necessarily a thing of grace. There was no sense of body rhythm. The angular arms flapped and the spindle legs kicked. She reminded me of something, a stork.

When she was married to Frank Sinatra, she invited me to her home, I was immersed in anxieties. André was again away conducting the Houston Symphony. Why aren't you with him? she wondered. There's this terror of flying, I confessed. Of crashing. And if you crash, so what? she said. It's your only life. Live it today, don't worry about tomorrow. It was easy for her to say. With that infuriating youthful remoteness from death. In an effort to win points in my favor, I confided to her my real fear. André didn't like to be alone in strange hotel rooms. I used to try to keep up with him by train. Then trains began to appear as monstrous to me as jets. My nightmare, I told her, was that one day someone would hold out a hand to him. And out of loneliness, he would accept.

> beware
> of young girls
> who come to the door
> wistful and pale
> of twenty and four
> delivering daisies
> with delicate hands . . .

The last time I ever saw her, she came to our home with Liza Minnelli. It was one of those evenings I'd read of in books. There were just the four of us. André played, Liza sang. Every obscure song she requested, he knew. Liza went on about how thrilled she was to have such a renowned accompanist. All the time, Mia sat at the far end of the room, politely listening, quietly observing. In contrast, Liza's effusiveness began to seem like gushing. She kept touching André. Possessiveness ate at my gut. And that night, when Mia and Liza left, I angrily resolved Liza would not come again.

They say all that's not said is known. Now, I believe the one who walks out the door isn't necessarily the one who leaves. We rush to collide with fate. And if some of us are sluggish, grounded beings who can't move fast enough, there are many willing to help us ahead in order to keep the date. Their aid comes delivered as gifts wrapped with deceptive ribbons. Sometimes the present we felt we least needed turns out to be the one we wanted most from them. Them? Who the hell were they? Who incessantly asked me how I knew all *they* said was true?

> goodbye goodbye
> no time for tears
> no time to wonder why
> goodbye reply
> my younger years
> yet i can scarcely sigh . . .

chapter 14

Of what use is a lyricist without a composer? Very little. But I kept putting words on paper. Even locked in the bin. More revealing words. Why not? I had nothing to hide. No one left to protect. I brought a cheap guitar. It would be a struggle to write my own music, but if I were to go on with my more personal style, it was a necessity. Several composers had read the new lyrics; all had turned them down. One close friend was honest enough to say that along with losing my mind, he thought I'd lost my talent. Do you want to write songs? he said. Or do you want to express yourself? I wanted to do both. Even if that self expressed could only be identified by crazies such as the patient who thought he detected the language of reds.

That patient had been convinced that while he slept the CIA had planted a bug in his head. He constantly held a small radio to his ear to drown out his thoughts and fuck up their bug. I had my own version of an inner voice and wrote about it in "Mr. Whisper." A group met in the day room. I sang the song as an admission. The nurse asked if anyone else heard voices. Lillian, a woman who hadn't spoken since they brought her in said, Yes, I hear a voice sometimes. What does it say? the nurse asked. All sorts of things. Like what? Lillian looked down at her hands and murmured, It says, don't eat the meat, or I'll kill your child.

i was riding in my car
screaming at the night
screaming at the dark
screaming at fright
i wasn't doing nothing
just driving about
screaming at the dark . . .

In 1959 I wrote "Control Yourself," appropriately recorded by Doris Day. In 1968 I wrote "Twenty-Mile Zone," appropriately recorded by no one. It was decided I'd have to record it myself. I sang it to a woman friend. Her face went bloodless. You can't reveal that about yourself, you musn't let that out! she said. Well, it happened to me, I said. I'm willing to take the risk. She did her best to dissuade me, claiming some things must be kept secret. But I felt the song would help to make that sort of thing acceptable. I tried to kid her, saying I'd bet that within five years the whole subject would be a cliché. I was wrong. Within *two* years it was a cliché. Eight years later, Paddy Chayefsky discovered the power of screaming in his script, *Network*. Three years earlier, the woman with the terror of self-revelation died of cancer. She was thirty-eight.

Oh, my fair Pastheen is my heart's delight,
Her gay heart laughs in her blue eye bright . . . .
                                    Samuel Ferguson
                                    (from an Irish folk song)

chapter 15

Something could be said for the longevity of writers.
They seem to have more *shelf life* than actors. The last
Academy nomination came for "Come Saturday Morning," written with Fred Karlin. Within less than a dec-
ade my work had spanned a musical generation from
mother to daughter. The song was for a film called *The
Sterile Cuckoo*, starring Liza Minnelli. Alan Pakula, the
director, told me he needed the lyric fast. Written in a
couple of days, it was based on two kids looking ahead;
the weekend symbolized the unknown tomorrows.
Alan loved it, particularly the title. Then came a hurried
phone call. He had decided to change the movie into a
memory piece. He wanted me to rewrite the lyric into
the past tense and still retain the title. Alan, I said, the
title is about the future. Alan empathized and was
adamant. It was a good challenge. With careful rewrit-
ing I kept the future title. The song ended with a word
indicating the past. *Gone*. The last word lingers, the
tense is set. André was in London.

He wrote a letter of congratulations on the song. He
wondered if we could continue to collaborate. If I was
willing, he was. At the end of the letter he asked for a

divorce. I said no to the continued collaboration. In reply to the request for a divorce, I said yes. He divorced me. He had the better grounds. His indiscretion was less than mine. He left me for another woman long after I had deserted him for another reality. He stuck with me in the snake pit beyond the endurance of many. I recall him conquering his own apprehensions to play the piano in the day room for the crazies while they twitched and picked at themselves. He became acquainted with some of the other inmates. He could laugh with penned-in adults who found humor in imitations of barnyard animals. Our actions may have been termed disturbed by some, but he understood the joke. His natural optimism convinced him I would overcome my malady. Eventually even his optimism was defeated. To this day, I don't know how he stayed so long. It's a tribute to his gullible heart. Not even at the end, when I hated him most and wished him dead and buried, did I feel he'd given me more cause to grieve than I gave him. But to the bitter finale, open discussion was impossible for us. While we were still living together, I learned of his affair on the TV news. A phone call from a newspaper columnist told me he was to father a child. A great many people heard as casual gossip through the media, the painful truths exchanged by two troubled people incapable of confronting each other privately.

I made a final attempt to reach André. Flying had been out of the question for me. But I tried to take a plane to London. And again wound up in the cuckoo's nest. About a month and a half later I was again let out on a pass to attend a meeting — the Sandpipers' scoring session of "Come Saturday Morning." Liza Minnelli was also going to record the song.

Liza made a request. Through Alan I was informed there was one word to which she objected. It was in this line:

> . . . and if it's gay
> we will stay.

I'm very interested in archaic language. Words should be revived and restored. Nowadays, *gay* is a word with a singular connotation. To confine it to a description of homosexuals is limiting to the word and to the people called by the word. As a predominantly heterosexual person, I feel discriminated against when certain words are off-limits to me. So I thought I would resurrect *gay* and use it in its original poetic sense. Meaning lively, merry, sportive, also beautiful and fine. I told Alan my resentment and assume he told it to Liza. In any case, the objection prevailed. The word was striken out.

I began to concentrate on writing and recording albums of autobiographical songs. After the first blundering attempt to steal the melody of "The Whiffenpoof Song" I taught myself musical composition. Though there have been some TV assignments, I've not done a movie since. Strangely enough, the last film offer I had was not as a writer but as an actress.

chapter 16

Milos Forman told me of an incident in the story department at one of the studios. On the desk of an editor was a stack of my albums. Milos wondered why. The editor explained there were movies about the Los Angeles earthquake, the *Hindenburg*, the *King Kong* remake, the Hollywood Sign. And that I had already written and recorded songs about those subjects before any of them was made. Frankly, she said, I'm looking through the albums hoping to find another potential idea for a movie. Milos and I discussed this. He said I should look over my stuff and beat them to it. I searched the albums, and began to create a script based on the song "Moon Rock." The title was *Genesis Rock*.

In 1965, my friend Bob Klein published a book of my lyrics. Included was a song entitled "Hair." In 1967, two years after that book came out, the musical *Hair*, opened in New York. When I finished the script of *Genesis Rock* I sent it to Milos, but didn't hear from him. Later I learned he was involved in directing the film version of *Hair*. With my usual luck, I thought, *they* had beaten me to it again.

When Milos was preparing to direct *One Flew Over the Cuckoo's Nest*, he startled me by asking me to test for the part of Nurse Ratchett. That was a terrific compliment to the former tap dancer. I went with him to see a stage production and was appalled. The Nurse had been drawn as a completely one-sided person. She was cruel, sadistic, without redeeming features. That's how Ken Kesey chose to represent his central female character. I respect his writer's choice. To play a character, it's not necessary to be in agreement. If you're an actor.

When an actor is cast in a role, it's a foregone conclusion he's playing a part. The audience accepts him as being someone other then himself. But when I see Paul Simon on screen I know *first* it's Paul Simon. If he goes on to play other parts I'll begin gradually to accept him as a player of roles. But when only one part is involved, the writer must be sure the role he plays doesn't contradict what he presents in his writing. I don't refer to songs written for other characters. I refer only to autobiographical songs. Nurse Ratchett, I felt, gave the lie to everything I'd written. To play her would have gone against my principles.

One night some people were at my house for dinner. Someone mentioned a movie that was shooting on location in which everybody in the town took part. The mayor, the priest, all the local tradespeople, even the undertaker. Everybody agreed there wasn't one person in the world who, if given the opportunity, would refuse to be in a movie. Oh yes, there is, said Milos. And we're sitting in her house. I began to have regrets. All my principles went out the window. What an asshole I am, I thought. But I couldn't admit it to Milos.

When he won the Academy Award, I called to congratulate him. He asked if I'd seen the film. I hadn't. He told me to go and see it. To see what I missed out on. When it was in second run, I finally made myself go to the theater. Louise Fletcher was amazingly good. I can't imagine any other actress giving a better performance. As for the role of the Nurse, I hadn't the slightest regret. She was plain rotten. I knew I'd been true to myself to refuse. Yet in a terrible way, that Nurse was as much a victim as McMurphy. And more of a minority figure than the Indian who escaped to a small measure of freedom and the faint possibility of hope.

> it's two a.m.
> i cannot sleep
> i pace the halls
> someone is calling
> help me . . .
> it's two fifteen
> i sit in fear
> i have a guard

R. D. Laing refers to those who "decide to embark on a career of schizophrenia." But what of the technicians, carefully separate in their uniforms of command and control? What compels those neat intruders to nest in the sick littered confusion of the cuckoo's alien home? It is said, the cuckoo lays its eggs in a nest formed by another bird, by which they are hatched. Put another way, the eggs are hatched by a stepmother. The wicked stepmother who's left with the responsibility of another's brood and brooding and who tends to them as her own. McMurphy was cast by his parents into the nest of another. The Nurse was equally cast off by her parents. In the alien nest he furiously sought to play the son. She bitterly tried to impersonate the parent. Both were defeated by the lies of their lineage.

Recently I read that McMurphy was considered by some to be the hero of this generation. If so, then Nurse Ratchett is the back side of McMurphy's frontal-lobotomized head. And all the more tragic, since she's doomed to remember and not be permitted to understand the murderous mother role she elected to play in the *suicide* of her bogus stepson.

> *Who knowes, but in the Braine may dwel*
> *Little small Fairies; who can tell?*
>> Duchess of Newcastle

chapter 17

Insanity is terrific on the Late Show, André once said, but in the real world it's shit. But the real world *is* the Late Show. And both reflect symptoms of the malady of the twentieth century. We leave Olivia de Havilland writhing in the snake pit and fade to the commercial. Where a used-car dealer is standing on his head or wrestling with a heartbreakingly dignified animal. Better that than Olivia? Of course. He walks free and comes on strong. She's locked up, and scared of her own shadow. He's easier to deal with. His is the more familiar type of madness.

It's not easy to visit a mental ward. Rarely does anyone show up, outside a patient's immediate family. And they spend most of their time glancing uncomfortably at their watches, or reading the paper. A lot of them do the crossword puzzle. Two friends of mine, Judy and Don Quine, were kind enough to come to see me. They had a good healthy interest in the place. With permission, I took them on a tour. Of course the lock, the straps, and the shock-treatment rooms are kept to themselves like embarrassing questions. Later Don confided he hadn't been too apprehensive. Except he'd had this weird feeling someone was going to jump at him from behind a closed door.

> i laughed
> and reassured him
> the techs are always on guard
> one sign
> of a patient's violence
> they move in
> hard
>
> but
> i had seen
> a face in a doorway
> i recalled when they had gone
> a boy hid
> behind don's shoulder
> the boy
> i'd seen
> was don.

The closed door is a potent symbol to the inmate. I used to stare at the wood and see faces in the grain and eyes in the knotholes. But every child sees those figures. I'm sure they are the basis of elves and gnomes. The difference is, when you're a child the creatures symbolize the free flight of your imagination. When they re-emerge to an adult, on a locked door, the entrancing elves become ogres. Reminders that for you there is no exit.

> leprechauns
> are upon me
> elves are
> showing themselves . . .

One of the great foolish terrors of being confined is the possibility of being seen on the street by somebody you know. When you're taken on an outing, you're not permitted to stray from the group. There you are, two by two, trotting behind the attendant. Like ducks. You can't wait to get back in. There are social workers who work free of charge distributing coffee and cookies to the patients. Larry, another patient, found out those Grey Ladies got together and the one who drew the shortest straw was designated the loser, stuck with a week's duty in the crazy ward. Our loser showed up pushing her cart, her smile as stiff as her hair. She carefully picked her way along the corridor, making a conscious effort not to touch or be touched. Obviously the poor woman was petrified. But her fastidious revulsion angered us, since she couldn't take her eyes off us. As though she were dreading and hoping something God-awful would happen. Unlike in the movies, mental patients aren't particularly overt in front of civilians. You're constantly being observed or listened to. Privacy is out of the question. Anybody could have your fate in his hands. When an outsider comes through the locked door, tremendous will is put into acting *normal*. But to Larry and me, the Grey Lady's behavior was as insane as the used-car dealer's. We decided to give her something to stare at.

The next afternoon the day room was unusually quiet. She entered warily. Suddenly Larry leaped up and crowed like a rooster. I flapped my elbows and quacked like a duck. The Grey Lady dropped her cookie basket and got the hell out of there. We congratulated each other on our performance. The next day *I* would be the rooster and *he* would be the duck. We laughed. Then we got sad. We knew the Grey Lady would never even notice we had changed roles. Only that we were *different*. But we weren't different. What she saw was an agreement. Some people got together and mocked up an answer to the question of what constitutes crazy. Then those people agreed to forget the unanswered question and settle for the mock-up. Crazies, blacks, midgets, roosters, pigs, dogs, ducks, males, females. Those aren't different, those are mock-ups of difference. Ill-defined as angels or devils. As elves or ogres caught in the door, they are victims of interpretation. Images strung of a common thread, cross-grained, ingrained, against the grain, yet, forever bound together by the wood of a single tree.

> i walk in
> i ain't too dumb

i know i got some
handicaps t'overcome
i mean y'seen one midget
y'seen 'em all
oh yeah midget
oh yeah small
and that's as far
as you can see
is that the sum
and total substance of me?
midgets d-warfs chimps in a zoo
they all look alike to you.

chapter 18

For years I'd been requested to perform my songs. I was
terrified to appear in public. But people kept writing
that my songs were *down*. That they lacked a sense of
humor. I was defensive, convinced they were funny. I
felt if they were performed the audience would respond
to the humor. That challenge made me decide to *come
out of the closet*. Shortly into my first concert at UCLA
the students giggled, at first a bit embarrassed. As the
evening wore on they warmed up. And when I came to
"Twenty-Mile Zone" they clapped in tempo and
roared. We acknowledged a common demon and dealt
with it by laughing at it. Demons take themselves very
seriously; they don't stand a chance against a good
belly laugh.

I've gotten lots of letters about that song. The best was from a high school student. He and some friends were playing it on the beach and singing the chorus. Along came some adults who scolded the kids for screaming and acting crazy. The kids said they weren't crazy. They were very sane. And in fact, another adult had written a song about screaming. They played the track. The elders listened. When it was over they said, Well, if its on a record, I guess it must be all right. Media validation.

My fourth concert was scheduled for Carnegie Hall. I was scared to travel to New York. What if I flip out in the dining car? I asked Mike Nichols. What if you do? he replied. Don't you see the joke, Dory? Your fear is you *might* go crazy in public. But since your story has been in print, you're free to be a freak.

People will accept your insanity. It's been given *media validation*. (At that time, Mike was in the middle of directing *Catch-22*.) The strange thing is, once Mike convinced me it was okay, I didn't do it. Couldn't that apply to all of us? If we gave ourselves and each other permission to act out our worst fears, would we continue to feel compelled to act them out? Would we keep needing to test the lines of strict conformity? Would those lines eventually be necessary at all?

> well along comes a motorcycle
> very much to my surprise
> i said officer was i speeding
> i couldn't see his eyes . . .

When I began singing the verse of "Twenty-Mile Zone" a motorcycle passed Carnegie Hall. Its siren going full blast. The audience broke up. So did I. We had to stop and begin again. Later, the fusion of the three elements struck me. Outside, a stranger starts a siren, inside, an entire audience reacts, and onstage, the performer stops a song about a siren. The concentration of four thousand people is irrevocably split by someone totally unaware of the impact of his small coincidental gesture. But was it a coincidence?

chapter 19

> crossed connections
> lost connections
> empty corners,
> crowded intersections
> accidents, incidents
> we're children of coincidence and fate . . . .

I finished writing that song just in time to keep an appointment. I got in my car and headed for my destination. At a crowded intersection I stopped. Cars were lined up in all directions. As I waited in line for the light to turn green, four cars plowed into me. Three of the cars involved were driven by relatives of people I knew. I've wondered if my intense concentration on that lyric had something to do with that experience. Had I attracted it? I was the only one who was injured.

Are we responsible for our own injuries, whether we're wounded by ourselves or by others? Reluctantly, against all my conditioning, I've come to suspect we are.

Everyone is partly their ancestors;
just as everyone is partly man
and partly woman.
Virginia Woolf

chapter 20

The best thing about a song is its brevity. The worst thing about a song is its brevity. Often a statement cries for the other point of view. Of course women have suffered from being in the shadow of men. But what of the man? It's a tremendous burden to be expected to cast a shadow big enough to accommodate two people. Gladly I placed that burden on him. Expecting him to open the world for me. I thoughtlessly put my heart into his care, settled cozily into his shadow, and made him responsible for my life. *He* was life. *I* was him.

> i lived your life
> till there was
> no me
> i was flesh
> i was hair
> but *i* wasn't there . . .

In the beginning it's great for him. The ultimate compliment, to have a woman who imitates him, follows his every gesture, echoes his every word. But after a while it gets like that kid's game. The one where your best friend repeats everything as soon as you say it. At first it's fun. You laugh. She laughs. Then the game is over and you say, Stop it. And she says, Stop it. And you say, I'm not joking anymore! And she says, I'm not joking anymore! Then you yell at her, she yells at you and you run away. And she stands there, hurt that you left her because of a stupid game. You watch from a safe distance, wondering why she took the game so far. If she'd only stopped eating at you, maybe you'd have stayed. Would you have stayed?

No, he was right to leave. I'd have taken the game way beyond far. Much as I'd like to quit, I can't bring myself to surrender. The pig-headed Irishman hangs in there, a real sore loser. And when there's no life left to feed off, I lock myself into an antiquated dining room and silently gnaw at myself. But hell, even a sore loser can't stay locked in forever. I'd tried to be him too long. Once I was convinced my man was gone for good, I determined to develop my own manliness. I would become my own man. The coward would scare up some courage. Men flew, became kings and presidents, went to the moon. I would strengthen my manly self to compensate for the weak, crazy sister. My efforts paid off. My albums gained recognition. Several of them made *best* lists. People were starting to notice me for myself. I was someone. On my way to somewhere.

chapter 21

the africans say
the soul fades away
with every picture
they claim
in five hundred years
when the soul's disappeared
the face is still
the same. . . .

Someone called to say Lord Snowdon was in Los
Angeles for an exhibit of his photographs. He wanted
to take my picture. Well, a guy who was not only English but had lived in the palace could make mincemeat
of a New Jersey mick. Besides, I hate to have my picture
taken. When he called I told him so. He assured me
he'd make it very comfortable for me. And the next day
he came to my house. New circumstances, new rooms,
especially new people make me shake. I was afraid he'd
notice. When he took my hand I felt him shaking as
much as me. Are you nervous? I asked. I'm terrified, he
said. That mutual honesty led to a fairly relaxed afternoon of shooting. The next day he had the pictures developed and the following day two of the pictures were
added to the exhibit.

His photos included a diverse variety of subjects from a
great white whale to Tolkien. The exhibit spanned
twenty years. Next to each picture was a card profes-

sionally printed with the year and the month taken. Next to my picture was a piece of paper on which Tony had hastily scribbled: TAKEN YESTERDAY. I connected the phrase to my fear of being photographed. Many things, some real, more imagined, have been taken from me. The most deeply felt loss was self-incurred. At seventeen. When I had that first abortion.

chapter 22

Only after I'd left the chorus of the touring show did I find out for certain I was pregnant. Impossible, I said. I've never even had an organism. Orgasm, corrected the doctor. Would you fix it? Absolutely not. Tell your parents, they'll stand by you till you have it. In those days there were no free clinics and no legal way. So it was done in the style of a B movie. In a seedy Hollywood hotel room. The fetus was flushed down the drain. Along with the lyric and the first love-letter.

It took me years to get up the courage to confess my sin, compounded by the second abortion. I took great pains to angle for a measure of understanding and forgiveness. Figuring it might be more lenient with straying sinners, I chose the New York actors' church. Inside, I searched the name plates for a priest with a kindly Irish monicker, something akin to Barry Fitzgerald. To top it off, I picked Christmas Eve. I pulled myself together, went into the booth, and confessed. The kindly mon-ickered father went into a black Irish rage. He accused me flat out of being a murderer. If I had taken those children, he said, and bashed their skulls on the con-crete sidewalk, I couldn't have been more guilty in his eyes. He raved on further, about how, People like you store up your filth all year long. Only to desecrate his sanctified ears during the holiest season. He muttered a hurried penance and ordered me from his sight. There was no point in staying to hear Mass. I left the Church for the last time, an ex-communicant. Outside, I stepped from the curb onto a sewer grate. I looked down through the opening. A faint ribbon of dirt-gray steam filtered through the accumulation of refuse and rose like some displaced, dancing soul.

Twenty years later, a nurse opened the door of a locked room and saw someone crouching naked in the toilet bowl. The person was trying to flush herself down the drain. What in God's name would make her try such a thing? She and another nurse discussed it as they tried to pull me out. I didn't want to be evicted. I stiffened. Get the doctor, she's going into catatonia! A few lines of an old song crept into my split head.

> catatonia, catatonia,
> what makes your big head
> so hard . . . ?

I laughed like hell. Listen to that, said the nurse. What reason has she to laugh? No reason. That's what consti-tutes crazy. They laugh for no reason.

Kilroy was here!
  World War II graffiti
  (Author unknown)

chapter 23

the way
that one behaves
is determined in the graves
of all
the great-grandparents
gone to dust . . .

Early in life, I claimed regret at not having had children. I no longer delude myself with remorse. There's now no desire to leave behind an heir as a bid for immortality. We're all desperate to leave a mark. A book, a picture, a child, something to show *we have been here*. Of the easier marks, I've come to think making a human life is the most egotistical and the least responsible. I shrug when people say, It's going to be different with my kid. Or, My child won't make the same mistakes I made. Of course he will. Through our children, we expect a brighter future, liberation and change. They won't change. Because they've been cut down to fit the shape of our unchanged patterns. In order to change the design, a pattern must be self-recognized, admitted, accepted. The self, not the heir, must be torn apart and reconstructed.

When I was nine my mother got pregnant. When a sec-

ond daughter was born, my father again refused to recognize her as his own. I hated his rejection of her and
secretly liked it. Later, when my father did accept her I
imagined she "took" him from me. I grew up bewaring
of younger sisters. I promised myself I'd never allow
that to happen to me again. Imagine my disbelief when
my husband was "taken" from me by a younger girl.
Once more, pregnancy was involved. This one resulted
in the badge of the fertility pill, the multiple birth. After
I was divorced, I fell in love with the man who produced my records, Nikolas Venet. We were making
plans to live together when he told me a young girl was
to have his baby. He would have to stay with her, of
course. Of course.

> do you think you'll get married?
> i ask in my worst
> artificial rehearsed
> type of voice
> eat your chop suey
> he orders then answers
> she waited too long
> and i don't have a choice . . .

Well I raged in the manner of Greek drama. I cursed all
baby-makers. Why did they always do that to me? I
anguished so long over why and wherefore, a vague
shape began to press through the self-pity beclouding
my mind. There was a *pattern*. Whether or not a sister
actually took my father was unimportant. If one girl actually made twins in order to take my husband, if another girl made a baby to take my lover was of minor
concern. The only important thing was, it had hap-

pened *three* times. Don't you see, dummy? No. I resisted stubbornly. It was them. *They* did it. Finally, I faced it. The pattern wasn't theirs. It was *mine.*

chapter 24

daddy boarded up
the dining room
and locked us in
we three
four and a half months
we lived in that room
my mama the baby and me
my mama slept on the table
i slept on a cot
the baby was in a basket
i hated it a lot. . . .

It's been said, it takes three generations to produce a schizophrenic. Half a lifetime of analysis convinced me there'd been too many psychological scars to have tolerated any pregnancies. Had I given birth, I'd surely have passed my patterns on to the child. But cutting into one's body to attack a fetus must be considered barbaric and transitional, till more sensible solutions are found. Education is imperative. When my sister was born and also rejected, our sick father locked her and me away in a room. He symbolically killed two children. I had two abortions. I killed two children. I was only acting according to my father's instruction, obediently following his blueprint for behavior. As a result of ignorance, I'd permitted the first pregnancy to proceed close to five months. I didn't tell the doctor. He gave me an injection and told me to count backward from a hundred. I counted. He felt my abdomen. But you've let it go too long. I can't remove this fetus. How long have you gone? I heard him ask. I kept on counting. Refusing to answer. Terrified he'd change his mind. It was too late for a quick abortion. Dilatation was performed. I went to a hotel to wait for the miscarriage to relieve me of the fearfully unwanted fetus. A woman sat with me in the hotel room. It was a long wait. In pale imitation of my mother before me, I lay on the bed in labor more than twenty-four hours before letting go of my own unwanted child. I felt something follow the fetus. What is it? I screamed, fearing another life. It's nothing, the woman assured me. Only the afterbirth.

Education has enabled me to make a choice. To take the responsibility for not having any children. But knowing how to prevent pregnancy wasn't enough. For by then, I was able to cut into my own mind. I'd read all those books, learned all that intellectual stuff, and still hadn't really changed. Demons pursued me. Guilt possessed me. Education works only to a point. After self-education must come education of *self*.

It's altogether possible a child could have coped with the weight of my sick patterns. But what about me? I was an aging embryo. Would the baby have ended up taking care of the mother? And what if the mother decides to leave, as her mark, the act of suicide? The self-destroyer has no further problems with this world. But the suicide's child is imprinted with another pattern to add to its already staggering burden. And another three-generation cycle is put into motion.

My analyst once told me a child with one parent can do very well. A child who suffers the real or imagined loss of both parents is bereft of substance. I call that child a shadowless being. The shadowless being decides how much substitution the loss will require. Marilyn Monroe was fatherless, then her mother was *put away*. Marilyn never had children. She didn't create a child in her own image. She created a shadow in her own image. A shadow of such cinemascopic magnitude that it blotted out the being who created it.

chapter 25

> mine was a bloodless death
> not grim not gory
> more like ali macgraw's
> new enzyme detergent demise
> in "love story" . . .

Most creative women commit bloodless suicide. Sappho, Virginia Woolf, Sylvia Plath, Anne Sexton, all suicides. Emily Dickinson, the Brontës, victims of death by self-entombment. Neat and tidy, they pass away, undramatically, unheroic. Those women weren't heroes. Heroes bleed, they don't kill themselves. They troop off to war on their Achilles' heels with our welfare tucked in their tunics. Then they embarrass us by coming back alive. Heroes make ass-holes of themselves by sticking around to bore us telling and retelling the tale. Janis Joplin, Billie Holiday, Marilyn Monroe? They weren't heroes, they were idols. Idols don't bleed, they crack. They fall from their pedestals and are crushed under the weight of the crown. Perhaps those women died for something, recognition, fame, a man. But I doubt it. Only men die for something, God and country, honor, the team. Men die for each other. Women die for themselves.

I suspect women have no compulsion to troop off to war because they are not obsessed with the sight of blood. A man's blood must be spilled. Exotic games must be invented to enable him to watch it run. A woman's blood flows. Peacefully, in her natural home, every month. Yet many creative women commit bloodless suicide. Why? Perhaps it doesn't have to do with death, but with birth. When a man gives life to a child he gives into the woman. But he gives *up* nothing of himself. Giving life to his creative art follows the same pattern. On the other hand, a woman gives birth to a child through labor, pain, and blood. She gives up *a part of her body*. When a woman gives birth to her creative art she's programmed to make a sacrifice. His war is his blood. His art is his life. Her child is her blood. Her art is her death.

Sometimes "masculine" men commit bloody suicide. With a gun or a knife they spill their own blood and watch it run out. Like a deserter. Yet we like to believe it's *un*masculine to desert. A hero's blood wouldn't dare run out. It would stay at its post where it belongs and if everybody's blood stayed put and protected its own home front, there would be no more war. And everybody knows that's a typical crazy woman's idea. It's us against them. Never us against us. We must agree on that. Why must we?

Agreements can be broken. It's done all the time in war. We never yell *foul* during battle. Any male act is justified long as our teams wins. But in peacetime, a broken agreement is considered dishonorable, unheroic. Rather than disagree with her peaceable feminine programming, a woman bent on sacrificing herself to her art is forced to take unnatural measures. So most women, creative and otherwise, kill themselves by depriving their blood of oxygen through pills and gas ovens, drowning and sealed rooms. Their instinct is to stop the flow, never permit it to run. That means those women *were* heroes. Ah, but we agreed.

> some reds
> are like familiar friends
> they spring from the growing earth
> they flow with the moon
> and tides some reds
> are the badges of brides
> and birth . . .
>
> some reds
> are unnatural enemies

they crawl out of open veins
they creep
and slide from gaping wounds
like medals of pride
and pain. . . .

chapter 26

The child is simply a reflection of its parents. Two people come together and make an image, a mirrored image, a reflection of themselves. A reflection casts no shadow of its own. If both parents lock it out by real or imagined means, the reflection fears it will fade away. And it will. For it is nothing but a shadowless being.

The shadowless being frantically runs to find someone else to look at it. It feels it can exist only in another's eyes. And can appear to be present only in the shadow cast by someone else's substance. If all substance is taken away, the shadowless being fears the jig is up. It had better leave a mark fast. Better still it will *make* a mark. Then perhaps the mark will see it. Or the mark might return some of its lost recognition. So the shadowless being begins to make stuff. Sometimes a shadowless being imagines it is watched over by Someone Unseen. If it decides the Unseen Someone is wrathful, it invents weapons of defense. If it decides the Unseen Someone is benevolent, it creates art to praise and give thanks. Depending on which parent it wishes most to replace, the shadowless being calls the Unseen Someone God-father or God-mother.

> jesus was a androgyne
> jesus was a he and she . . .

chapter 27

One night as I watched Marlon Brando on television, something stirred, a long-buried fantasy. If I could just meet Marlon Brando, I secretly felt he would take one look at me, I would take one look at him and our eyes would lock. In the background cheap movie music would fade in on a hundred and forty-seven strings. My hair would suddenly miraculously grow to my waist and it would be straight. I would run across the crowded room in slow motion, like a deodorant commercial. And he would pick me up in his arms and carry me *walking* across the water to Tahiti. I was the only one who knew how to handle him. A friend watched with me, Elizabeth Ashley. Feeling very singular, I described my fantasy to her and asked, had she ever had such a dream? All the time, she replied, all the time!

Brando symbolizes "hero" to a lot of people. Elizabeth wondered who was Brando's hero. Well, that's my style game. I'm intrigued with names and initials and how they can be made to relate. I ventured a guess, then pieced together some clues from his life to create a myth. When he was a kid, I figured, he might have gone to the local movie house to see the original *Mutiny on the Bounty*. Maybe he dreamed of living the part of a mutineer. And marrying a beautiful island woman. When he grew up he married Movita, who played opposite Gable. He went to live in Tahiti. He named one of his sons Christian. Even his initials correspond. Marlon Brando/Mutiny Bounty. He's lived his life as a renegade from the so-called ships of state, studio and governmental control. He identifies with the third-world minorities and ecology. But he did one thing few of us can ever do. He played the role of his hero, Fletcher Christian. When I wrote a song about him, I admit having hoped it might lead to meeting him. No such luck. I came close, though. When I played the Troubador in Los Angeles, a woman was introduced to me backstage. Jocelyn Brando. Maybe she told her brother. Probably not. It's just as well. Since then I've seen my hero play the role of the Godfather. If I ever met him one question would burn to be asked. Who is the Godfather's Captain Bligh?

chapter 28

The full picture of the Hollywood Sign always seemed to elude me. For years as I turned a corner, I caught a glimpse of it slinking into a palm tree. As I left the freeway it faded behind a gas pump. Playfully it edged into view only to be eclipsed by an Orange Julius stand.

An acquaintance invited me to his house for dinner. Driving up into the hills, I kept catching sight of the letters. As I got higher, the sign got clearer. My heart started to pound. I reached my destination, got out of the car, and stood eye to eye with it. Posing brazenly naked across a littered chasm. Run-down, in need of a new paint job. Some of the letters tilted dizzily. The brush at the base hadn't been manicured for years. Caught in the cactus about its pilings were condoms, empty bottles, an inner tire. Yet it had an air of mystery. A secret. Once demolished by real estate and quick-buck investors, that secret would go down with the sign. There had been rumors about a starlet who had jumped to her death. What was her name? Was she a dancer? The door opened. I said to my host, This is going to be a quick dinner. I've got to get home and write about that sign.

The starlet who jumped, I learned, was named Peg Entwhistle. What a melodious name. Ent-er smiling. Don't call us, honey, we'll call you. Sure, daddy, you're in charge. But if you need anything, all you gotta do is whistle. She's got you pegged. The most inexperienced little starlet knows what every man wants. But magnates, moguls, mythical kings, and Freud continue to ask, What is it a woman wants?

Peg was a girl who aspired to stardom. She wanted to move up in the world. Yet she killed herself by jumping *down*. Whom did she rush to meet down there? What illusion waited for her, crouching among the empty bottles and strewn condoms that tainted the chasm below?

> when mary cecilia jumped
> she finally made
> the grade
> her name was in
> the obituary column
> of both of the
> daily trades
> i hope
> the hollywood sign
> cries for the town
> it touches
> the lady of lourdes
> in her grotto
> saw fewer cripples
> and crutches. . . .

> *The new ideas go far beyond*
> *Darwin's concept of apelike ancestry*
> *for man; they pursue the path of*
> *evolution backward in time from*
> *our tree-dwelling ancestors to*
> *the first forms of life on the*
> *earth; across the threshold of life*
> *and into the world of inanimate*
> *matter; then farther back, to a*
> *time when the sun and earth did*
> *not exist; and farther back still,*
> *always asking: Why? What cause*
> *produced this effect?*
>
> Robert Jastrow

chapter 29

Part of me felt if I could answer that question I'd beat that built-in determination to die and make a new name for myself by living. I had come to settle in California. The edge of the continent. Land of the lemming. Where you've got to either start again or end it all. With a flying jump into the Pacific. And I can't swim! Other displaced Easterners sometimes ask why I've never lived at the beach. To them California seems to be synonymous with the sea. But for this Easterner it's an impossibility. Though I was born and raised near the Jersey coast, we never could afford a car and I was taken to the seashore less than four or five times. Our family considered swimming an activity of the rich. To this day I feel as foreign to it as to a tennis court. David Wolper hired me to write a song for his documentary film about ecology, *Say Goodbye*. Bob

Klein loaned me his place near the ocean for a week. Being distrustful of vacations I decided to write the song during my "rest" to give me the illusion I hadn't left home.

> when i was a child
> i ruled the earth
> i owned it all
> its total worth
> each fish each field
> each flower each butterfly
> then one day it occurred to me
> if i own the earth
> then the earth owns me
> and each of us must live
> or both of us will die . . .

The writing was difficult. One morning I took my guitar out on the beach and sang to myself what I'd written. Not only could I not hear my guitar, I couldn't hear the sound of my own voice. I laughed and couldn't hear my laugh. I looked at the ocean, the sky and the sun. How could anything we have to say be of the slightest importance? Suddenly a school of whales drew curves on the straight line of the horizon. I watched them play, secure in their own environment. Then I went inside, packed my bag, and went home to finish the song in my tiny, cluttered office. The sea and open sky intimidate the murky little mind of the bog-trotter. Great spaces are scaled to accommodate great brains. Such as is inside the head of the whale. I take an active interest in the protection of that gentle giant. Sometimes I fantasize they are macro-minding our planet. Wouldn't it be the final irony if man, with his fanatic regard for technology, is killing off the senior citizen of all computers?

I decided I might be able to go to England for a concert tour. Mainly because Joby Baker, the man I live with, agreed to accompany me. I am incapable of traveling alone. The plan was to go by ship. Before we left I had a nightmare, the ship hit an iceberg. It was so real I wanted to cancel the tour. I had to have help and returned to analysis for several weeks to work on the fear. Assurance was given, I wouldn't be alone. Joby said he would help me get through it. I explained frankly, without euphemisms, what might happen. He accepted the possibility. Therefore there were no surprises when I began to be gripped by dormant demons. Joby allowed me to face them *in his presence*, not by myself in a tower. In Ireland, I told him I encountered a ghost. He said yes. In England, I admitted to terrors of old countries and new stages. He said okay. In Scotland, I said, I don't think I can go on. He said, Then don't. So of course, I got up and went on. But I decided that would be my last long journey. It's enough for one to have such stress without laying it on another. I'm grateful to his patient often impatient tolerance. But the fearful reality is that, surrounded by others, we travel alone.

Autographs are part of the ritual of public appearance. Whenever I signed my name I wrote the initials S.T.W. Explaining to every person that they meant Save The Whales. They're an endangered species. Please pass it on. Just before the tour was ended we read headlines, a ferryboat had hit an iceberg. No one was hurt. I felt relieved. The dream had come true without harm to anyone. But on the return trip I was very nervous. Two nights out I woke sweating with fear. I'd dreamed again we hit something. I was unable to go back to sleep. Early in the morning we felt the ship go into a strange series of vibrations. We got dressed and went to find a ship's officer. He told us the ship had hit a whale.

How often I cry for that creature. Why did it rise from deep waters refusing to respond to its own sonar warning? Surely it had an appointment with every one of us on that ship and altered the course of our lives. In some ways we're unequipped to understand, we owe a debt to that whale. Often as I'm about to go to sleep, I give thanks to it for an unfathomed gift. Never again will I eat a slaughtered animal. Or buy a coat fashion-cut from an animal's skin. Long submerged ley lines were followed by fish below and ship above.

A collision is just a more dramatic version of a meeting. You may ponder your route to a certain person. What led you to him? By which primitive sense were you able to recognize him? An incomprehensibly complicated arrangement of corresponding patterns, natural/ unnatural selection, sounds, vibrations and clues. Have no doubt from without and within, prior arrangements were made. And what led *him* to you?

chapter 30

if i hadn't made a left hand turn
if you hadn't made a right
if i'd waited just a moment more
if you'd missed the light
if that car had never blown its horn
if that friend had stopped to talk
we'd have never met at all. . . .

It was seven years since I'd been in that restaurant. A business lunch with a lawyer whom I saw that once and never saw again. From across the room came one of my dearest friends, Robert Carrington, only recently returned from years of living in London. Through an English friend he was meeting an artist; they were going to his studio to see his work. After lunch, would I come over and join them for coffee? Elfin karma was at work again. Robert and I had prior connections. Some of them were missed.

I'd made one last attempt to fly to England in an effort to salvage my disintegrating marriage. André had sent Robert to the London airport to meet me. The plane arrived. Robert was informed by a stewardess that Mrs. Previn wasn't aboard. There had been some bizarre behavior just before takeoff. It seems Mrs. Previn had torn off her clothes. Then she ran down the aisle and screamed at a fellow passenger, a priest. What did she say to him? Robert asked. She threatened him, said the

stewardess. Threatened him? Yes. She had to be removed from the plane. Where did they take her? The
stewardess didn't know. They put her in an ambulance
and carried her away. Did she resist? Was she crying?
Robert asked. No, said the stewardess. She was *smiling*.
I laughed to myself. Finally I understood the joke. I
hadn't wanted to make it across the Atlantic then as I
didn't want to go across the restaurant now. I refused
Robert's kind invitation. He wasn't surprised or de-
terred. A while later he sent a note, again I refused. On
my way out, he got up and stood between me and the
door. We had coffee, the artist arrived late and was introduced, Joseph Noel Baker, called Joby.

Elizabeth Ashley always kids me. Well, you may fancy
yourself a *lady of letters*, honey, she says. But to me
you're just Dottie, the ex-chooo-rine! That day, Dottie
saved my ass. It seems the artist was also an actor and
former nightclub comic. The writer and the artist didn't
get along, at all. But the chorus-girl and the comic were
able to see through the masculine/feminine disguises.
Our masks had worn thin. They were too threadbare to
fool another loser. Cruel truth filtered through the
cracks. Cruel truth was what attracted us to each other.
Since I was too old to be regarded a female prize, he
responded to the man in my heart. Since he was too
poor to be judged a male success, I was drawn to the
woman in his soul.

It might seem presumptuous to refer to another person
as a loser. But Joby and I have discussed that at length.
We came to the conclusion the winner compulsion is all
cocked up. For when you're a winner and you some-

times lose, it's *devastating*. But if you're a loser and you occasionally win its *fantastic*! Just when I gave up on men, felt I had left that arena, Joby came into the restaurant, looking defeated by his own overwhelming losses. But something in me must have known this was a fantastic win. Why else would I have avoided him so long? I gave him every version of no on my vocabulary. The loser in me fought tooth and nail till finally there was dredged up, as from a thoroughly gutted archeological dig, one last furious yes.

> you're not dealing now
> with no mere winner
> someone who's never learned
> how it feels to take a fall
> you're dealing in me with a loser
> that's the strongest opponent of all . . .

I am often attracted to the female side of a so-called masculine man. I regarded it as a compensation for my own weak female side, the crazy sister. I cherished my masculinity as my savior. The rational side that kept the possessed woman from falling prey to demons and enemies. As long as I was manly, *they* couldn't touch me. I felt very apprehensive about forming an alliance with Joby. Because the more I worked on strengthening my constructive side, the more a feeling persisted, someone was trying to do me in.

> i seem
> to see this stranger
> almost everywhere
> i do not wish
> to frighten you

but you should know
he's there
so that if you're threatened
if evil's ever done
you'll know
it's him who did it
you'll know
that he's the one. . . .

chapter 31

sing glory to the golf balls
that were driven across her breast
she was a very gracious hostess
to a most ungrateful guest . . .

If it does take three generations to produce a split child, perhaps the same is true of generations. We're each a reflection of the whole. Is it possible there is a relative process to produce a schizophrenic generation? During this century we split the unsplittable atom. Later we followed the moon's pattern and split from the earth. Now we talk of splitting to other galaxies. Would our encounter with another planet be a meeting or a collision? Would we go there as enemies or, worse, as friends bearing gifts typical of our technology, pollution, viruses, golf balls and Tang, stranglers, flashers, and related undercover operators? Beware of younger planets bearing gifts. Arriving all smiles and political sweet-talk to lull the spacemates into a sense of well-being. Eventually to become once more *us* against *them*. But I suspect they're way ahead of us. Older and smarter, they probably could have blown us to smithereens an eternity ago. But they already know what we suspect. Attack from the outside is no longer effective. Head-on confrontation is passé. Man-to-man combat obsolete. Bombs, guns, knives are old-fashioned. Prisons are ineffectual. We no longer need to render a person impotent by locking him in a cell. We have split the cell itself. Why should anyone attack us from without when we're doing the job on ourselves from within?

In my opinion, madness is a microcosmic demonstration of the twentieth-century malady. It is a disease of the center. The center cannot hold because it is already split. We have broken *atomas*, the indivisible. We are an atom divided, a self divided, a house divided. Now we threaten to become a planet divided. Vagrant, vague, wandering, incoherent. Schizoplanos.

> we split the atom
> we split our minds
> then we split (from)
> the whole damned planet . . .

Well, I didn't want to split. I'd already done that. Space intimidates me. I'm too nervous to fly over the cuckoo's nest. I preferred to stay put, yes. *In my place.* My planet, my home, my snake pit. Cuckoos and snakes have very foreseeable patterns. I would probably be stung in the ass or get bird-shit on my head, but it would be my fault, not theirs. My paranoia was growing, with my luck the planet would be blown up before I figured out who was trying to do me in. I had to uncover my enemy within. Time was running out. The awful voices were starting at me again.

> . . . last night
> i found obscenities
> scrawled across my wall
> i swear
> i can't repeat
> the filthy words that i recall
> and then
> the most immoral
> damned insulting thing of all
> as i read each line
> i noticed
> his handwriting
> was identical
> with
> mine.

The cuckoo is a pretty bird it sings as it flies
It brings us good tidings and tells us no lies
It sucks the young bird's eggs to make its voice clear
And the more it cries cuckoo the summer draws near.

(Irish folk song)

chapter 32

In my grandfather Patrick Shannon's old Irish patter
songs, the cuckoo's nest meant the *pudendum muliebre*,
in other words, the shameful cunt. Was it possible the
one I thought was my weakest link was in fact, my
strongest enemy? I examined the idea. If I'd been a
man, I'd have had it made; instead I broke just like a
woman. Just like a little girl, I'd gone cuckoo. Of course!
The villain was the shameful cunt, the mad bitch! It was
her or me! But I was too tired to win another fight. The
woman had done her best to sacrifice herself through
pills. The hero was too taken with his brand new
masculine tunic to soil it with blood. It was embarrassing to have had to admit that I wanted to survive. To
write myself to death. Like the Irish drunk in the tavern
who tells and retells his tale to himself long after the call
is announced. Thus in keeping with the humiliating
will to live, I decided to surrender to the enemy, the
crazy sister. I would go *on my own* to live in the locked
tower. With her. The inner enemy. My sinister side.

Once done, I set out to learn to co-exist in enemy territory. Become familiar with the crazy sister's patterns instead of suppressing them. I learned my enemy was smart, a regular J. Robert Oppenheimer. Over and over she'd run test implosions. The ragged desert of my inner hemisphere was barren, near burned out. Before she made of me a total wasteland, a radical change of patterns was indicated. Instead of continuing to believe the reactivator was trying to do me in, I altered my reaction. I chose to believe she had not been trying to destroy me, she had been trying to get *through* to me. She'd been breaking me down to keep me from killing both of us. What monstrous blame I'd laid on her. If I acknowledged that responsibility perhaps my reticent woman-self would graciously grant my ambitious male-self the patience to tear loose the stitches from the destructive patterns and find buried beneath other lost threads of reconstruction. And common growth.

But it took three generations to produce this genius of self-destruction. How does one go about freeing the elf from the wood grain? Where do you begin? Books, old records, relatives, through a knothole in the family tree? That would mean traveling once more across the sea to the home of my Irish ancestors to face the grim reality that the moss-banked river Shannon is polluted by its own split, occupation, outer advancement and inner strife. I'd have to push this un-*see*-worthy dinghy-dory against the stream, then trot my meager craft across the unfamiliar swamp where all know the Banshee lurks and if I were lucky enough to escape to the hilltop, wouldn't it be to find at the source it's a circular trip trickle trek swell fell trip trickle trek swell well it's a fact, hell isn't it a fact that the outflow of the once gay and green river was never naught but the gray and mean Atlantic and on the way back we might hit another whale? No.

The network is too vast, patterns too complex, stitches too tightly interwoven of old threads and older knots. But suppose I were to take one thread. Less, one strand of one thread of one stitch and try to pull it loose. Untwist, unravel, untie till it made a kind of sense. Any kind of sense. Un-sense, in-sense, non-sense. The strain of madness has caused in me a genuine lapse in taste, I've come to prefer a fool's order to an intellectual's chaos.

So then, which strand shall I choose? Narrowed down, the only craft I'm practiced at is writing. That's too broad. Words. Narrower. Letters? What kind? Initials! Since childhood there's been that obsession. Creating words of them to make images of the words. To convince myself of the mock-ups of angels, idols, elves, guards, keepers, cells, split cells, destruction, death, worse, the loss of my immortal soul. But since I and my newfound enemy had agreed to stop trying to destroy each other, we would reverse our trip. Away from death and head back. In the direction of birth.

> . . . left-handed people are impure
> they go against the grain
> left-handed children
> play with themselves
> and drive themselves insane.

"I love my love with an H," Alice couldn't
help beginning, "because he is Happy. I hate
him with an H, because he is Hideous. I feed
him with — with — with Ham-sandwiches and Hay.
His name is Haigha, and he lives—"
"He lives on the Hill," the King remarked
simply, without the least idea that he was
joining in the game, while Alice was still
hesitating for the name of a town beginning
with H. "The other Messenger's called Hatta.
I must have two *, you know — to come and go.*
One to come, and one to go."

Lewis Carroll

chapter 33

I'm a member of the Rosebud generation. Citizen Kane's story ends with a word. The camera wanders back over his life's journey, the lost sled leads to the one who gave him the gift before he was taken away. An aerial shot of his vast storehouse. The camera eye moves as over a map till it finds its target. It zeroes in on the name printed on the burning sled. The letters melt, too late for Kane. But not too late for us. We have seen the word and have made the direct connection. Every seemingly unrelated scene in between suddenly falls into its logical place. Was it the same in "real" life? Are there visible readable patterns? If one could split from oneself, rise into the air and see the life's journey from the beginning to the present time would it form a logical connective design? If so, it isn't random, there are rules to the game. What game? I have no idea.

Among other things, critics accuse me of self-preoccupation. Right. I have nothing more important to do
than play with myself. I decided to make up my own
game. I called it Initial Origins. The initial I chose to
begin with was B, for born. Next, place of birth followed
by parents' initials, grandparents' initials and my own
initials. They totalled fourteen. Then I made a list of
fourteen people in my storehouse who seem at the
present time to have had the strongest influence on my
life. Fourteen out of twenty-six letters in the alphabet.
My mother told me I'm stupid at numbers, so I can't
figure the odds for or against coincidence. The important fact was, *not one person* had initials outside my
own initial origins. I wasn't too surprised. But I was
completely thrown by the incredible conclusion of the
game.

INITIAL ORIGINS

a game invented by Dory Shannon

Born: New Jersey

City: Rahway

Mother: Florence Shannon

Maternal Grandparents:
Nora Kenneally, Patrick Shannon

Father: Michael Langan

Paternal Grandparents:
Anne Trainer, Nicholas Langan

Original Name: Dorothy Veronica Langan

Names	Influence	Corresponding Initials
Florence Langan	younger sister	Florence Langan
Alan Baron	first boy-love	Anne Born
James Barrie	first affair	Jersey Born
Arthur Barrett	first lived with	Anne Born
Leon J. Bronesky	first husband	Langan Jersey Born
Robert Schneideman	first teacher	Rahway Shannon
Arthur Freed	first writer contract	Anne Florence
Norbert Raymond	first analyst	Nora Rahway
Nathan Rickles	second analyst	Nora Rahway
André Previn	second husband	Anne Patrick
Mia Farrow	André's lover	Michael Florence
Nikolas K. Venet	lover after divorce	Nora Kenneally Veronica
Valerie K.	Nikolas' lover	Veronica Kenneally
Joseph N. Baker	now living with	Jersey New Born

chapter 34

From *Born New Jersey* to *Jersey New Born*. I was seized by a rush of Catholic fervor. I am reborn! Euphoria was followed by a swift descent into the pits. I'm not reborn, life is a rerun! We keep going back to the beginning and replaying it. Till we get it right? Not only is it a rerun, it's a foreign film. A Technicolor musical with subtitles and dubbed voices. To understand the plot we've got to watch the action, listen to the music track, catch the lyrics, and read the dialogue. All the while we're struggling with that, the original language is registering subliminally, like some kind of aural X ray. I felt an old, familiar panic. Was it an omen? Augury? A *true* Hollywood sign? Control yourself, Dory.

If it's all been shown before, why the hell are we here in a theater that endlessly runs only one feature that's been produced elsewhere, possibly elsewhen? If that's the case, the movie isn't foreign. *We* are. A maddening possibility. Repetition is so boring. But think a minute. At least we're involved. All dancing, all singing, all talking. Maybe if we start to listen carefully, watch the lips moving, we might learn the language. Then translate the songs. Break down the color patterns. Analyze the same old story, find out why it's always the same old *fight* for love and glory. Let's question the direction, roles, actors, techniques, make-up, costumes, disguises, subtext. The projector, screen, seats, popcorn concession, theater, audience. Hey, whose theater are we sitting in? Forgo that for now, that's a galactic issue. There's too much going on inside with this retread, reissued, rerun, replay. Hey, play it, then play it again.

But you can't recognize the players without a program. And as the rerun continues, a phone call comes. I pause in writing. Joby has come in to say he's cast in a small role in a movie. He will have to interrupt his drawings for this book to leave for location. The female star is Mia Farrow.

> i lie in bed
> beside him
> and unravel him like twine
> i know his depths his drives
> his drawbacks
> as he knows mine . . .

A short time ago I'd have collapsed to show him my weakness. But he knows my weakness, as I know his, so there's no longer a need to collapse. We can't control arrangements previously made, only our reaction to them. Instead I laugh with elfin karma and tell Joby to go ahead and trembling wish him well. I console myself with the truth, human beings can't be bound. Our only security lies within ourselves. We've agreed there's to be no marriage contract. With a legal bond one is not free to leave, neither is one free to stay. Without a contract we're free to leave but also free to stay. Then I deal with the trembling, remnant of another old pattern. She may be attracting herself to me but am I also attracted to her? Pulling in possible threat, playing Russian roulette of the heart? Probably. But now I know I'd react differently. If a woman were to threaten my home, this time I would deal directly with her. When it comes to minor skirmishes, I've grown into quite an effective minor adversary. It's the major encounters that continue to knock me out in the best sense of the phrase.

Joby dabbles in the game and has already seen that his two ex-wives, Joan and Joyce, had initial origins in common with his own. And then there are his two daughters, Michelle and Frederica, and his stepson, Scott. Are those three Jewish children distantly related to the Irish Michael and Florence and Shannon as well as closely related to Joby born Joseph Noel as in Jersey New baby sister Florence whose confirmation name is Michelle and is my mother, Florence, related to Joby's father, Frederick, as well as to his mother, Frieda? Play it again and pay attention and maybe the scattered clues will begin to connect eventually to fit together as tightly as the closely woven silver screen on which the patterns are projected.

> play it sam
> play it again
> take me back
> to you know when . . .

chapter 35

Initial Origins led to other discoveries. The similarity of Baron, Barrie, Barrett, Bronesky, Baker. Then, before Joby, there had been the Greek Nikolas Venet, named the same as my dead Irish grandfather Nicholas and my favorite Uncle Nick. The game was conceived one night when, as usual, I was waiting for Nik. On a piece of paper I wrote his first initial, N. Then my two husbands' initials, André and Leon. Then the initial of my first boy-love. Together the four letters spelled out his name, A-L-A-N. Then Nik arrived and I forgot that game for a while.

Twelve years younger than I, he was street-smart, tough-talking, uneducated. At first he referred to me as the Beverly Hills lady. Ironically he only saw me as the image I'd mocked up for myself. And he resented it bitterly when I taunted him, saying under the counterfeit license cowered a beaten mutt just like himself. I thought I'd finally settled for someone lower down,

closer to my origins, he was my last chance. At my age,
I couldn't be choosey. I did all the older-woman clichés.
Showered him with gifts, loaned him money, and, for
the first time, was the sexual aggressor. My first truly
passionate attraction. I became hooked on him as I was
hooked on pills. I didn't want to be seen in public with
him, then went into a fury when I learned he didn't
want to be seen with me. It might have been because of
the difference in our ages. Several times I'd watched
him drive by with a lemon-haired girl at his side. My
position was ludicrous. The former wife of a man with
three paragraphs in Who's Who, for Christ's sake, was
reduced to the clandestine mistress of an unmarried
man. But Nik had redeeming qualities.

Child of the sixties, he understood madness and drugs.
He looked into my eyes and saw through my behavior
when I was stoned. He openly referred to it and did not
judge. I was alternately filled with hatred for him and
gratitude that he allowed me to be my own confused,
insane self. Added to that, he considered my work the
best songs he'd ever been given to produce. A tiny seed
of trust took hold, I began to confide in him. He listened and identified with my experiences, the aural
hallucinations that refused to let me be. There were two
more confinements. After that, I dropped out socially
and narrowed my world to the few people who could
accept me without my cover. Those occasional times
when I crossed over into the more social world I com-
prehended a growing change. Sanity, unreachable perfection, mythical kings were no longer my preoccupa-
tion. I told Nik my aspiration, to be a spiritual beast. To
try to develop my spiritual self while recognizing and

accepting that my roots were planted in the muddy bog.

How stunned I was later to discover Nik also had a secret life. He was far from beaten. Away from the world of pop-media, he lived another style. He was a collector of Indian art, his house was filled with treasures he'd bought with little money. Well read on the history of Indians, he counted many as his friends. There were pilgrimages made to ceremonial grounds, hallucinatory experiences shared. He was welcome in some of their homes. John Neihardt was an acquaintance. I gave Nik an Indian ring which he brought to Neihardt, and when the old man died, it was buried with him. Nik was changing. He rented a house at the beach and came into the city less. He went into therapy which gave us more in common, constructively. We grew closer spiritually as well as physically. Hesitant plans were discussed. Finally there was the tentative agreement to live together. Then he fathered Valerie's child.

> he's at home
> among the homeless
> singing set my people free
> he will march
> with total strangers
> but he will not walk
> with me.

There were no partners left for me. That's when I decided to quit the male arena entirely. This time *I* would be the rooster. From lame duck to cock of the walk. I fell in love with another woman. She showed me a new kind of understanding and consideration. Yet even in that nourishing relationship I felt relegated to the weaker position. She was tall, and when she stood over me old patterns led me to feel cast in the powerless inferior role of woman. My legs were too stumpy, I was too short to effectively strut along that walk. Still caring for her deeply, I withdrew. It was difficult for both of us. In the end it was her manliness I couldn't cope with, not her womanliness. Or more accurately, was it my womanliness I wasn't yet ready to accept, whether homosexual or heterosexual? Something fell into place.

My father was certifiably crazy. My mother was an incurable martyr. They battled continuously. It seemed my father always won by sheer force. I didn't understand then that a martyr can be stronger then a madman. I imitated the battle of my parents. My head was split into two warring opponents. But I had reversed the roles. One side was the male martyr, the other side was the crazy female. Both sides were weak, without substance; their constant bickering drove me mad. Seeking sanity, I had strengthened my male side, which only drove my threatened female side crazier. Surrendering to the crazy female strengthened my womanly side, but threatened my male side. When the aggressive man tried to take over completely, the assertive woman rebelled. I had actually rooted out and recognized the two roles I played. At last, I was able to clearly define my inner turmoil.

> so i hereby take myself
> my soul doth take my heart

> to honor love and cherish
> till death do us part
> i will
> i will accept myself
> with hope and fear and wonder
> and what i have joined together
> let no one put asunder.

Life was lonely, but with work I achieved a fairly stable female/male balance. There was as yet no outer partner, but I had an inner partner. *We* could make it alone, together. The two parts of me were finally united. At peace. The voices would stop forever. Late one night, coming home from a therapy session, I made a spontaneous left turn against a warning signal. I considered ramming the sign, instead I put the car in reverse, then went forward around the warning and drove down the trafficless street in the wrong direction. Suddenly I swung off the pavement and found myself trying to drive along some obsolete railroad tracks that ran parallel to the one-way street. I pushed the car till the wheels spun. They were caught between the ties. I could go no farther. I'd been stalemated.

*Until finally the chain of cause and effect
runs out, and the trail vanishes.*

Robert Jastrow

chapter 36

please doc
don't let them
give me shock
i ask you
don't blow my mind
with a block . . .

There was another breakdown. All the self-confronta-
tion had been to no avail. Acceptance, recognition were
mere wordplay. Responsibility wasn't a matter of
choice. The most stubborn resolve was ineffectual
against *softness* of the head. There was nothing left to
do but stop dead in my tracks, and give in to the creep-
ing catatonia.

Without making a conscious decision, I locked myself
up. In my own house. And prepared to go through it
alone. It was worse than a split, I was fragmented. One
side argued, threatened, railed against another side. I
screamed at the voices to go away and begged them not
to leave me. If one could hang on, remain alive, the
most virulent disease finally burns itself out. Why then
couldn't mine? What kind of monumental sickness was
it that could rage at peak energy for over twenty years?

The fever subsided, I lay exhausted, yet recognized the walls of my room. Somehow I'd managed to reorient myself. The worst had been gotten through without help. That in itself was a victory. Then, I began to question. What if those voices gave me no peace not because they were sick, but because they were healthy? What if all those years had been spent going in the opposite direction from the cure? If it were true, that would mean all those guards, techs, nurses, doctors, all those learned experts with their degrees, all of them were *wrong*. Impossible. A colossal case of self-inflation, I'd been there before. But hell, I'd tried everything else, why not try a reverse procedure? There was nothing left to lose. But there was. Something I didn't want to admit even to myself. It was this: always when I went round the bend, I'd been able to get back. What if I went out to meet my voices, surrendered myself to them, and they held me there, trapped for all time? Was I about to walk into bondage? Was this the only thing left for me? To hopelessly lose my mind? There was another alternative. Instead of confronting them on their turf, I would ask them into mine. I would accept their madness. I decided not to return to therapy. And quit taking all pills. If I was to live in another reality, I must behave myself. Create a good environment. Select carefully.

> . . . weapon or gift
> enemy or friend
> how a world begins
> is how a world will end.

I politely invited the voices to come in quietly. A welcome was extended, they were free to exist in my head.

The door was unlocked, I was willing to make them a part of my reality as long as they behaved themselves. I meditated every day. After a long period I learned my first lesson. *They* had decided to accept *my* madness. A sensible dialogue would be possible only if I behaved sensibly toward them. My inner friends had finally gone past me and gotten through to myself. The door was being unlocked to me, I was the one being set free. I had come back and instead of leaving them behind, I had brought them back with me. Still today, when I open the inner door, my mind scurries around like a pig in their parlor. But my inner friends are patient with my lack of evolvement. They wait till I stop listening to my own boring reruns and settle down. The oinking subsides and I pay them attention like an obedient child. As one newly learning a language, I mix metaphors all over the place. I don't care. Anything to free myself of preconceptions. For when I forget about my lamebrained ideas and concentrate on *them*, they give me affection and courage and instruction. Now I travel along a finely balanced line. With one head in fantasy and one head in reality. I won't say which is which. But I am *able to travel.* No longer do I feel so alien in the twentieth century. As long as I listen, am watchful, and ever on guard, I'm bound to be sure my inner friends love me. At last we are integrated.

> you will become entangled
> in the simultaneous vision
> of sea floors
> and far stars
> one eye pointed up and out
> the other pointed down and in

and your
self
groping stunned and unbalanced
between the two . . .

chapter 37

On a recent summer day I sat in my kitchen and watched a grounded bee make its way across the floor. It came to a hair-ball shed by my dog, Scylla. Instead of side-stepping, the foolhardy bee confronted the hair head-on. Within moments the bee was completely entangled. At the far end of the kitchen, Scylla slept. Unaware of the life and death struggle going on with a piece of her discarded fur.

But the bee was a noisy little bastard. Its buzzing eventually roused the dog. She got up and followed the intrusion. She moved closer to the struggle. Not too close. A sensible dog, she keeps her distance from hysterical bees with indiscriminate little stingers. She watched for a while, then trotted away. I picked up bee and fur with a piece of cardboard and deposited the opponents outside. By the time I came in Scylla had already gone back to sleep. But I was glad she noticed the struggle.

I watch her sleep. Her feet begin to twitch. She dreams of herding her flock in an earlier time on an ancient plain. She is a Hungarian sheep dog and for want of a meadow or mountain will shepherd me into the car or onto a chair. There she sits with her rump on my foot to protect me from the ogre who howls at the back of her dream. Expectant, she sniffs at the L.A. air for a whiff of magyar threat. The enemy wolf inscribed on the center of her genes. But why is the word *enemy* stamped on every cell? Who is the crazy who must be fought and locked away? Why does this *false* monster lurk in the ball of hair? In the knot of the wood-grain? In the bog of the brain? *Demanding* to be recognized?

"Are you animal—or vegetable—or mineral?" he said,
yawning at every other word.
"It's a fabulous monster!" the Unicorn cried out, before
Alice could reply.
"Then hand round the plum-cake, Monster," the Lion
said, lying down and putting his chin in his paws. "And
sit down, both of you. . ."

Lewis Carroll

chapter 38

. . . and whatever happened
to roses, to roses red and wild
the kind that grew
in her grandmother's arbor
when she was a child
when the monster smiled?

A bit before the beginning of time there roamed in the dark and murky swamp, one terrible two-headed monster. It had a pair of male-eyes staring in one direction and a pair of female-eyes staring in another and a monstrous mid-section holding together the two opposing forces. The other animal-creatures all of whom came in pairs, viewed the singular monster as dangerous, disorderly, and pitifully lonely. Relentlessly searching for its partner. Incapable of thinking its way clear to its other self. It couldn't see it was its own partner. Alternately one head raged while the other head wept. Not only had neither head ever confronted its twin, it was utterly incapable of meeting itself even halfway.

The divided vision caused such conflict within the monster's mid-section it ran in all directions, cutting down everything in its path. Till finally on a desecrated plain it ran blindly into itself. It met itself coming, going, and sideways. The collision's impact was felt throughout the swamp. The other half-eaten, down-trodden creatures sadly rejoiced. The monster who'd fucked over all of them had finally fucked itself.

The bashed-in smashed-down knocked-out knocked-up monster lay where it fell. Gradually it felt in its mid-section, a strange growing stir. It was the potential to love. The monster would never again be lonely. It grew so excited it got up and danced with itself a monstrous tarantella. It got so caught up in the dance it forgot the initial reason for its glee. Its whirling twirling became so uncontrolled it caused the blessed event to arrive prematurely. The other creatures watched woefully the scene of the death and the monster's despair.

The two-headed monster crouches over its child. The mid-section smells the death throes. The fetus writhes, sucking toothless at receding life. There is a spasmodic grasp at air. Life manages to side-step. An attempt to leap is countered. And life leaves the fetus abandoned to its rapidly deflating umbilical sack. A sigh is heard. The monster is suddenly alert. It is merely the sound of the caul fluttering on the final expiration. The fetus in-nately turns away from life and follows the flutter. The child dies with its ears caught up in the sound. With its eyes fixed on the film.

> . . . this here child
> she's got two diff'rent eyes

one is dark and one is light
one looks out at the morning
one looks in at the night

The monster buried its breathless child in the center of the swamp at the base of a small fir tree. As the fetus was tenderly lowered into the ground, the umbilical cord was caught by a needle on a limb of the tree and the caul was torn from its other. The monster was so engrossed in the dead half-body of its offspring, it gave no mind to the slimy cap with the still pulsating cord. The pulse was sheer will. For the tissue had been interwoven with the same potential and had felt the same stir of love when it swaddled its half-born twin. Please don't leave me, the caul cried to the dead child. Come back, I love you. Stones covered the child's remains. All the while its twin, its wisp of the will, shed eyeless tears of fathomless grief. A cry was heard. The swamp resounded with the double echo of the monster's unbearable loss.

i'll hold the child
i never held
in a place
called yesterday . . .

The bereft monster left behind its dead child with its unrealized living potential to love and took to the mountain top. Two eyes scanned the sky above, two squinted at the swamp below. Caught between grief and guilt, it was soon unable to move in any direction. And dimly perceived it must make another move or die. But there was no outer escape. So each head inwardly agreed to forget it had trampled its own love-child to death. Slowly, through religiously practicing rituals, the monster trained itself to believe it wasn't mutually responsible. Whenever the painful subject arose, each silently blamed the other. More children were born to cover and compensate. All they did was bury the dead child deeper into the dark pit under a forgotten tree in the center of the primeval swamp. In defense, the monster cultivated a taste for all things perfect, shining, clear, and high. And developed a disgust for all things incomplete, dark, muddy, and low. To keep the uneasy peace, the mid-section consoled its gut reaction with aspirin and epicuria and went along with the lie.

> i have flown
> to star-stained heights
> on bent and battered wings
> in search of
> mythical kings . . .

Far beneath them, the shadowless afterbirth was in a bind. Hanging suspended from the fir by its umbilicus, the caul vainly sought refuge. The other creatures remembered the untrustworthy parents and instinctively refused to allow it the protection of their shadows. Naught was left for the caul but to make the best of its shortcomings. The cord curved the limb down, the sack slid onto the ground. The pulse stayed with the tree and tuned into the sound of the tree bark. The cap pulled off and related to slime and phosphorescence. It floated on stagnant pools and developed a taste for bacteria. It got carried away on the odor of musk. Slept under the stool of toads. And returned always to its own pulse, through which to take nourishment from the bark of its mother fir. Without arms or defenses it learned to live by its wit. And somehow the covert creature maintained below, at the base, bottom. Connected to the planet only by its own pulse, life was sustained in the caul, or as its archaic cousin is spelled, saul, of which the contemporary spelling is soul.

Yet it lived in constant fear. The monster might return and if the silent soul got in the way, it might easily be trampled or devoured as the other creatures had been. Who would protect it from the very one who'd given it birth? It missed the child unutterably. And lamented its lack of control over destiny. Actually it was connected by more than its own pulse. Its destiny was in the hands of another older ancestor, pre-monster, a great-grandparent named Fate. Fate is anciently connected with and distantly related to love. And Fate had come to the rescue. It stepped into the picture via the fir tree. The limb was the hand of Fate. The pine needle the finger of Fate. And the elfin humor of karma is best evidenced in the way Fate chose to protect the defenseless soul.

> . . . when the person was unraveled
> nothing stood
> where nothing stood before
> and the joke was lauded
> and the audience applauded
> more more more more!

In order to keep the monster from destroying its own soul, comedy relief was introduced. A cosmic joke was played. The one weak pulse of man's highest potential, love, had been deliberately left down in the dump.

Stranded, forced to fend for itself in the humid, fetid depths, the soul not only grew, it flourished. The crap and the cosmic became tightly interwoven with the vibration of the afterbirth strings and harmonized with the umbilical cord. Within the protective network the soul was perfectly free to cultivate its wit and humor. Not to mention an elfin love of the ridiculous and a flair for foolish jokes. Riddle me this! How come *no one* can destroy the soul? 'Cause *nothing* can't be destroyed, that's how come. Ha! Ha! If the pulsing cord is curved and interwoven with the tree bark, what are their real names? The warp and the woof. Heh! Heh!

Meanwhile, once a month when the moon was full, the two-headed monster would cast a substantial shadow from the mountain top. Then the shadowless nothing would drift onto the moonlit plain to dance between its parents' shadow and self. Look, it would croon in a cordless voice, I'm down here. And it would spark off the top of a triangle shaped root, or flash on the surface of a leaf coated with foxfire, or glisten on the saucer rim of petrified cow dung. The soul's store of childish antics went disregarded by the parents. Except once in a while, in a dream, when the tormented monster would try to escape the dark site of its dead child. Turning away one or the other set of eyes would spy something hung on a tree. An ancient umbilicus wrapped in the strings of its afterbirth, covered by a cap of its own caul. As the monster blinked back tears, it would shimmer and glow. The monster would applaud the faint light, then come awake lonely under the dark, distant night sky. The truth was the parents were so deeply scarred by the loss of their original child they were bereft of light. The monster was too weighty, all substance, all matter, ponderous. It had become a shadow-ful being. A substitute was required. The childless parents couldn't give rebirth to their original child. In its place, they decided to try to recreate the light.

> . . . sure that everything of worth
> is in the sky
> and not the earth

But it was the egg trying to lay the hen. The monster pursued the easier task and recreated the womb, a fertility mother earth. An agricultural figurehead to conjure the resurrection of the caul through the annual rebirth of trees and edibles. Greening, growth and grain. Then it created a replica of the dream umbilicus. Their omphalos was covered with the agrenon, the imitation network of afterbirth strings woven of the warp and woof of the wool of a sacrificed baby lamb and engrained with the seeds of life. Great new rituals were invented to lend pomp and circumstantial evidence to the light of the child. The monster's loneliness was not appeased.

Thenceforth in song and myth it was decreed that the imitation lost cord of the mother-head had the power to divinely will its own progeny into existence. That left the male without a father-head. The monster fought with itself through the divine children. Gods and goddesses vied in the monster's double head for premier umbilical position, head status. During a great migraine struggle the female head fell to the male head. The head-mother turned icy cold. The annual rebirth became virtually nonexistent. The rebuffed head-father turned into a head stasis. He became unmovable, unapproachable. The catatonic remoteness of the father figurehead reinforced the abysmal sense of loss in the dark primeval mid-section of the monster. Its heart was being broken. The shadowful being decided it would need more energy, more power, more light.

> . . . singing scraps of angel-song
> high is right
> and low is wrong

The rigid god-father-head convinced itself the blame for its plight lay within the frigid god-mother-head. She was to blame for the darkness within and without. The monster preached in temple and hymn that the god-head had fathered (through another illegitimate umbilicus) a pair of twins. Artemis, the girl, was the heart of matter. The lady of wild things, protector of the swamp, guardian of the black forest, perpetuator of the chase, goddess of all darkness. Apollo, the boy, was the soul of mind. The god of light, lucid, the Lycian, far-shooting archer, seeker, healer, master musician, poet. In whom there was no darkness whatsoever. Artemis had power but no *will*-power. Apollo had both, being decreed the umbilical connection between the monster and the divine light. He was the direct link to the enlightenment of the divine will. She was matter, he was mind. And all agreed it was mind over matter.

The receding glow of a forgotten dream soon haloed a completely motherless head. In that sisterless boy, the god-father-head created a light of such dazzling proportions the shadowful being could hardly see the god-son for its radiance. And still it was not enough. The loneliness grew to cosmic proportions, the fire had constantly to be fed. Ultimately the monster-parents were almost eclipsed by the nuclear nimbus they themselves had created to surround that first golden Apollonian head.

did jesus
have a baby sister
was she bitter
was she sweet?

New guilts developed. Two-head turned its attention to mature full-grown inventions such as devil's triangles and flying sorcerers and false-alarm fires set off by the myriad of unidentified objects and objectionable identities resembling one or the other head (depending on which one was objecting) that ceaselessly threatened its already overcrowded retreat. The monster combated threats by growing bigger, fatter, richer, higher and brighter to appear impregnable to the territorial/ terrestrial invaders. In so doing the shadowful being cast an ever grosser, more pregnant shadow. Till eventually, when the moon itself was exceptionally full with the second coming of Apollo, the monster couldn't help but recognize the great swelling spector darkly emerging from under its own two feet. To counteract the growth of its own shadow, the monster began to devour itself.

a great gray frog
now crouches
on the throne
of a former prince

and it's endless
croaking croaking
has no power to convince . . .

The mid-section tottered under the weight, trying to keep both heads balanced yet separate on the crumbling foundation of falsehoods. There was a gnawing yen for a lost potential. A remembrance in the overfed gut of that one brief stir of love. More and more frequently thoughts escaped and wandered nostalgically down into the swamp where they were eagerly picked up by the highly attuned, sensitive ears of the furtive soul. If its parents did return, the abandoned elf resolved to lead two-head on a merry chase. The monster would never catch the soul to gobble it up as it had gobbled everything else. Hah! Hah!

Because if there's one thing a shadowless nothing understands its how not to be devoured. Not by ascendants. Not by descendants. And most of all not by one's self. The trick, it could have told the monster, is to recognize yourself as what you are. Small. Not yet completely formed. Lower than toad-shit. Less enlightened than the singing whale. Less substantial than the sacrificed lamb. Darker than the dense pig. Slower than the horse. More senseless than the senselessly tortured rats spelled backward star same stuff as we are. Har! Har! Respect your true elders, it would say, recognize the force of the fickle finger of Fate or you'll get it rammed up your ass. Accept the position of underdog, exist on your bark not your bite, and forever be safe from threat, real or imagined. After all who'd want to eat such unsubstantial fare? A fool who dances on air?

One more thing then I'll stop dear parents on your
mountaintop I and my fellow animal-creatures down
here in the swamp are as closely related to the extrater-
restrials over your heads as the rats to the stars and beyond where ancient grandancestors call the tune of the
words of the singer I would croon if I had the cords but
Fate holds the cards and controls the whole game and
Spirit is Fate's other name so protect all those who are
beneath you and all those who are above will protect
you the child you once were knows what I claim to be
true and the present day child is about to be spoiled
and tomorrow's child will grow up just as dumb until
you comprehend that the children you two give birth
birth birth to will forget about me by the time they are
three so if you two bore a quadrillion or more the truth
would remain with the twain won't you see love was
left alas with the child of your past and the fool who
sleeps under the stool! Ho! Ho!

> the prince is charming?
> the dragon is alarming?
> the princess phony?
> the dwarf is true?
> they all hassle
> your head is the castle
> and all four characters
> are played by you!

There was a wee bit wifie,
Who lived in a shoe;
She had so many bairns,
She kenn'd not what to do.
She haed to the market
To buy a sheep head;
When she came back,
They were a'lying dead.

Mother Goose
(Scottish version)

There was an old woman
Who lived in a shoe,
She had so many children
She didn't know what to do.
She gave them some broth
Without any bread;
She whipped them all
    soundly
And put them to bed.

Mother Goose

chapter 39

alone in space
we together float
a frightened crew
in a fragile boat . . .

At the height of a contraceptive debate, a young jour-
nalist asked if I believed in the pill. Only as an interme-
diary step, I replied, until more sensible means are discovered. That's what you said about abortion! she
accused. If you believe both solutions to overpopulation to be archaic, what's your suggestion? My suggestion was will. Did I mean a woman could will herself
pregnant, she asked. Or not pregnant, I said.

In an ancient time women willed themselves to discon-
tinue the seasonal cycle as an evolutionary step toward
their survival. In the same self-interest, men willed
themselves to abide by the female discriminating. His

sense of smell lessened, he ceased to sniff out which-
ever women happened to be in heat. Mating became a
matter of choice rather than chance. But that choice
gave rise, I believe, to the illusion of love between men
and women. And that illusion eclipsed self-love. From
then on there had to be love *objects*. The primary object
became the child. The child-woman replaced the
strong-willed woman. Selective breeding became ex-
cessive breeding. Why the child?

When we were on a path toward planetary construc-
tiveness, why did the pattern turn into its opposite?
Why does multiple childbearing persist when it looms
as the prime contributing factor to destruction? Overpopulation means territory. Territory means invasion.
Invasion means my space against your space. And still
it is not enough. To paraphrase Freud, What is it we all
want? Well, to paraphrase my father, What does it
profit a planet to gain the whole galaxy if it loses its immortal soul?

> . . . illusions
> who touch in a trance
> making love
> not by choice
> but by chance
> we are shadows
> who dance

The child is the soul connection. Yet each of us dances
toward adulthood in such a frenzied tarantella, the rush
kills the very thing inside us which is related to immortality. Destroy the inner child and its twin is left up a

tree. The goal of the dead child is to be reconnected with its soul. Therefore the child wills itself to be reborn in order to *refind* its soul. We don't bear children. *Children bear us.* If each educated adult consciously resurrected, revived and *refined* the inner child, it would lead the adult back to its lost potential to love itself. If every parent matured, pregnant with its own joyful inner child, the soul-child would be creatively, constructively occupied with its present self. And its adult would not be pre-occupied with making future selves to recreate through nostalgia a return to that lost time wherein the past self felt that one brief stir of love.

If we change our destructive patterns today yes tomorrow's kids will be different, they and we won't follow our old paths. Paradoxically the future is in our hands, but the solution to overpopulation is in the hands of the children. The more securely reconciled the inner child becomes with its soul, the fewer future children will *demand to be born.*

How did a book of bio-lyrics get so far afield? Call it the bridge to my song. But is a lyric any less related to the universe than a Mother Goose nursery rhyme? Lyrics, jingles, poems, prose, and other outcries are as related to Mother Earth as the howl of the Beast is to Beauty.

chapter 40

the monster must be recognized
she hears her body shout
if we don't give it
dignity
this planet
is going out. . . .

Three years have passed since I wrote and recorded
my last personal song. Called "Wild Roses." At times
I write things I don't fully comprehend. Something compelled me to pick away at the subtext of that lyric. I was
determined to take responsibility for what my glib craft
had enabled me so easily to write. When I thought I understood what the lyric meant, I got scared. A transition
had taken place. Self-preoccupation had led to preoc-
cupation with the environment, another form of survival. And what's happening on this planet is, to me,
no longer anything to write a song about. Yet something continues to sing, doesn't it? The whale knows
something we don't know. Invaded, hunted, endangered, a part of its persists to sing in the polluted sea.
Under the sewer grate, back of a gas-pump, in another deeper part of the forest, something holds out
foxfire and croons in a cordless voice. I will forgo the
song for now and pursue the singer.

> *"Aren't you sometimes frightened at being planted*
> *out here, with nobody to take care of you?"*
> *"There's the tree in the middle," said the Rose.*
> *"What else is it good for?"*
> *"But what could it do, if any danger came?"*
> *Alice asked.*
> *"It could bark," said the Rose.*
>
> Lewis Carroll

chapter 41

In a world that reveres the dancer, I search for the singer. As usual, I'm out of step with the times. But I'm resigned to plod. And no longer aspire to learn how others fly. Marshall McLuhan said, The medium is the message. And through our technological leaps, we are jet-rushing to prove the mock-up true. Allowing the medium to tell us nothing, we encourage the medium to show us everything.

All our contemporary leading men fight, toot horns, shoot machine guns, fuck, jog, jitter, and dance. They behave, they never talk. On the other hand, their women never stop talking and say nothing. It's all wow, yeah, far out, right, really, la-de-dah validation of the mute attitudinizing of their men. And when they do pause to take a breath it's to segue into a reprise of a love song their mothers lip-synced adoringly to the contemporary leading men of the forties. Wait a minute.

There seems to be a pattern to these shadows who dance, these men who run, these women who repeat. Christ, is it going to be a rerun of World War I, coming home, settling down, sitting on the grass, under the shade of the old apple tree, waltz, buggy, spoon, marriage, diamond rock, lullaby, rock-a-bye baby, babe, oh-you-kid, Charleston, solo flight (across the Atlantic) celebration, crash, bread-lines, diners (greasy-spoons) peddling apples, the pits, grass-roots, depression, nervousness, jitters, jitter-bugs, boogie-woogie, bugle boys, marches, fliers, bombs, World War II, victory, coming home, settling down, let-down, unsettling, protest marches, activists, grass, meditation (pacific solo flight) flower-children, crash-pads, launching pads, rockets, moon-rocks, rock n' roll, roll with it, easy, soft, quiet, coke-spoon, drugs, hold, withhold, hide, spy, tape, tap, bugging, boogie, hustle, rush, attack, territories, terrestrials, atomic rockets, hydrogen reactors, reflex-reactions, reactivators, World War III, and don't sit under the apple tree with anyone else but me when the good ole' nuclear button's pushed, baby, is that the message? Well, I won't accept it.

Yes I will. I'll take the message but I won't swallow it whole. I'll digest every word before it goes down. I know we have the power to change patterns, reinterpret meanings. By taking a word such as reflex and turning it into reflects, we can find a constructive subtext in the most hellfire-and-brimstone threat. How do we begin? Well, we could read, library books are free. But that's too slow in our twentieth century. Well then okay, let's take just one word. Let's take it apart, untie the knots, isolate it from its connective threads and see if inside the expiring word we might rediscover a faint pulse. Of love. As I say I'm old-fashioned. I love a myth with a happy ending.

If this were my myth to recreate I would choose to forgo the message and concentrate on the medium. Dull word, medium. So middle-of-the-road. Average, without mystery, speed, imagination or flash. All its roots seem to stem from the one mediocre definition, middle-ground. No doubt about it, the word is a downer. But once upon an ancient time the medium was the oracle. The interpreter of the unknown to the known. Dealer in demon-rumor and angel-speak. The go-between shadow and self. Already we've found the smiling, level-headed, contemporary conservative is distantly related to the sooth-sayer, sweet-talker, cord-less-crooning, turd-glistening, swamp-dwelling collaborator with the full moon. Damn, you can't trust anybody, not even yourself. Especially not yourself. Paranoia wins. Might as well surrender to your worst enemy. Stop! But not to make your mind blank, to make it pay attention. Stop! Listen!

> i no longer plead with heaven
> or go rummaging in books
> for answers to the questions
> life contains
> now i listen listen
> listen to this inner thing resounding
> in the pulsing and the pounding
> of my infant ancient veins

Something is trying to get through to you. With different defenses against threat. Defenses so farfetched they could only be grasped by an atom-split, schizophrenic generation driven crazed by the awful realization it has the power to destroy itself. Things can't get worse, why not accept the fantastical possibility that construction might lie in the lost potential to love entangled in root, foxfire, and petrified shit. We all admit we scream, it's become a cliché. Now let's make a cliché of another truth. We all hear voices.

We've come a long way. In the old days we'd have been burned at the stake. Now we accept it as fact. We hear voices through telephones, records, film-tracks and TV. Why then, do we cling to the newfangled scientific hogwash that, within our bodies, all we respond to is the beat? There is more to us than music. There are words to the inner song.

All right. Once accepted, your inner voices won't be too terrific. They will rage. Wouldn't you if you'd gone unrecognized for so long? They will lead you on a merry chase, taking on the many disguises of the shift-shape. They will seek to identify themselves to one head as a mother, a goddess, the Virgin Mary, Artemis, the CIA. To the other head they will whisper they are Apollo, Napoleon, the FBI, Jesus. They might even threaten to kill your child. The child you once were who irresponsibly followed the elusive elf into the dark swamp. The parents in you will naturally grow protective. Don't put yourself through all that, you'll get hurt. They warn with good motive. For if you do eat the meat, that is, eat away at yourself, the child-ish-you will be killed. But it is the child-like-you which you seek. Just as with the heart, insanity has its reason. Madness itself is sick of all the rigid sense and longs to make peace with its restless soul. How may it be done? With great care and self-observation. If life is a rerun and we are in a theater, you must stop feeling you are being watched. And begin to become a watcher.

At age fifty-three I have again become an obedient child. Pupil of my medium. Listener to my Muse. I cherish the lost child. Baby daughter. The one I left buried in the bog. No longer am I wary of young girls. Part of me is a girl again. Natural twin of the *true* monster. My dwarf. Undiminished soul. Caul of the left-handed kid who plays with herself. Who drove herself insane. *And who hears voices.* Isn't it great? Yeah! And now we come to the catch.

Isn't there always a catch when something is caught on to? There is and it's this: Once you admit to hearing voices, you must admit that *the voices hear you. There are no secrets.* No more can we outwardly plead no responsibility for our words and actions without realizing our inner motives are heard. That's not so terrible if you've already admitted to damned near anything and everything and have little left to hide. Of course, it does give me an uneasy feeling of being held accountable to unseen others. But to me, that's a small price to pay to know I will never again travel alone.

> we were doing it together
> we were doing it together
> we were doing it
> together alone.

chapter 42

Take me, slap-happy medium, along the unbalanced, riddle-rutted, middle path of the perilous inner bog. On swollen, weary monster feet I stumble giddily behind nothing. Sticking close as a loyal dog. Pawing at stray bits of paper and worrying wisps of thread. Always alert to clues in the shape of coincidental spit and the stink of random spoor left behind by deliberate design to pattern the unpaved road. Lead me on, fool, then lead me on. To the oracle. For I admit I am lost. And the tiny beat of my heart cries to be accompanied by the majestic words . . . it sings.

chapter 43

> when i was a child
> she taught me how
> to turn the other cheek
> never start a row
> she said
> know when you shouldn't speak
> listen dorothy
> do be good
> an obedient child behaves . . .

No secrets? Okay then. Why *did* I write a so-called taste-less song about young girls? That's what I now am. More importantly, that's what I *was*. What I was too, was obedient. Turner of the other cheek. Trained to know when not to speak. What then was there in my well-behaved self that I'd publicly warned others to *beware?* As I said, I wrote the lyric to "The Whiffenpoof Song". Why did a high-school flunker choose that one to *borrow?* An old college drinking song, totally unrelated to the story told in the lyric, "Beware of Young Girls."

> We are little lost lambs
> who have gone astray. . . .

There must have been something I unconsciously knew and tried to hide. And, since there are no secrets the *tune* gave me away. The dictionary defines astray as, going into error or sin. Wasn't I once the younger girl who threatened an older woman?

My mother was right to get herself pregnant to defend herself from me. Dangerously close to puberty, I was going off every Saturday to dancing school with my father, her husband. A thief was in her very house, craftily planning to steal her man, by needle or poison pen. After which, the little crook would encourage *him* to lead her astray. What else can a father do with a girl except lead her into error and sin. Stuck in the craw of every man's daughter is the cliché question, If I were a boy would you feel that way about your image? Would you then want to play ball with me instead of wanting to ball me? Would you try to love me rather than fuck me?

Beware of young daughters who come to your bedroom door, they're love-starved and desperate to screw themselves into legitimacy in the shadow of your mythical king. And they're well-trained. By their mothers, grandmothers, great-grandmothers, they've been programmed to believe their only defense is to make another lamb, equally lost.

Experience has changed my original pattern in that regard. I now know there are other more loving, more thoughtful, less egotistical choices. Children must be born of reflection not reflex. In order to give them what *they* want. They must not be used as tools to get what *we* want. That late regeneration makes me no less responsible for my words and actions. If I hadn't been possessed of a well-founded primeval fear of the loss of my immortal soul, I'd have killed to get my god, my king, my father, her man. Surely, I wouldn't do in the very one who sacrificed a part of herself to grant me her most precious gift of life? Yes, I'd have even killed her. Don't forgive me, Mother. I knew exactly what I did. But I was deeply taken up with not breaking the Eleventh Commandment, Thou Shalt Not Be Found Out.

> two planes cracked up
> and fell into the L.A. sea . . .
> my mama said
> things come in three
> then i cracked up in L.A.
> and no one felt
> the crash but me . . .
> two planes cracked up
> so i did what i had to do
> forgive me pan am airlines
> for taking off
> but not with you.

Stealthily, I laid the groundwork for a massive coverup. Now I'm able to perceive somewhat how I covered my sin, blocked it, laid the blame elsewhere, imitated it with another married man, and hoped to Heaven I wouldn't be exposed. And when I wasn't found out by others, my old training to confess tripped me up and I exposed myself. Blew my own cover. When a man flashes in public, when a woman takes off her clothes in public, they're not exposing themselves. They're being exposed by their selves. I was on my way to London to make accusations about the adulterous "other woman" to my husband. But before I could do that I admitted my own adultery by exposing myself to everybody. By publicly confessing to the priest, for he was the father and was certainly wise to me. Bless me, Father, for I have sinned. I accuse myself of breaking the Seventh Commandment. Hadn't my mother always said the thought is same as the deed? And didn't I harbor grossly impure thoughts about her husband? On that plane I acknowledged my transgression. When I tore off my blouse before everybody I was *making a clean breast of it*. However, that action isn't to be regarded as particularly honorable. My motive was dishonorable. I called myself adulterer, I believe, only so as not to be accused of a far greater sin. Later the passengers said I'd hurled incoherent accusations at a complete stranger. A stunned priest. But in my confused mind, I saw that young priest as being distantly related to the old Irish father in the New York actors' church on that long ago Christmas Eve when I lost my soul. And I was terrified that, before all, he would echo his ancestor's accusation and call me *murderer*.

chapter 44

our fathers fight
through us
as they fought
their fathers' war
and the same old scene's
repeated as before . . .

and when i tell you
how i hate you
before the birth of jesus
before the death of caesar
before siddhartha
before ulysses
before the trojan war . . .

the feeling in my bloodflow
is a simple thing y'see
everything and nothing
in the parody is me
i'm the hero
i'm the villain. . . .

United we stand, divided we fall. We've been raised to
abide by that old cliché. But since the splitting of the
atom, I would like to heretically suggest that for us it is
now the other way around. Divided we stand, united
we fall. I was united by rigidly designed tightly woven
patterns. I fell. I had to divide the patterns into sections
to make smaller, more defined patterns. Every stitch is

distinct, but the whole picture made them seem indistinct. In attempting to separate and isolate one stitch I was endeavoring to specify the roles, identify the players, simplify the plot designed to work against me.

Once done, the fiercely united players were able to stand back from the conflict. They could stop grasping at each other and start grasping their selves. Only when they, that is, my selves were divided was I able to get out from under and stand up to *them*. On my own weak ankles. And how many pairs of ankles there are. I am a multitude! Does that sound egotistical? Perhaps. John Donne said, I should be mine own Executor and Legacie. James Joyce introduces the character H. C. Earwicker as Here Comes Everybody. Lao Tzu advises to, Abide at the center of your being; for the more you leave it, the less you learn. Why should I do less than follow their lead? And say with humility that I'm

> the beginning
> and the end
> i'm creator
> i'm destroyer
> i'm the enemy the friend
> i'm an animal
> a spirit
> flying high and falling down
> i am special
> i'm important
> i am sacred
> i'm a clown
>
> so i stumble through the chaos
> dragging clumsily behind me

all the eggshells
and the fish scales
and the fur pelts of my past
while this thing goes on
inside me at one with all
the vastness
the fantasies
and fictions
and when all the contradictions
come together
come together
they will fit
the feeling in my blood flow
is a simple thing y'see
i am it
I am it . . .

"What—is—this?" he said at last.
"This is a child!" Haigha replied eagerly, coming in
front of Alice to introduce her, and spreading out both
his hands toward her in an Anglo-Saxon attitude. "We
only found it to-day. It's large as life, and twice as
natural!"
"I always thought they were fabulous monsters!" said
the Unicorn. "Is it alive?"
"It can talk," said Haigha solemnly.
The Unicorn looked dreamily at Alice and said, "Talk,
child."

Lewis Carroll

chapter 45

the night was growing cold
the moon was getting dim
he sat there growing old
at least
it seemed that way to him
he waited past forever
to keep his love alive
but the girl
did not arrive.

Whenever I closed my eyes, during that solitary breakdown in the mid-seventies, I saw a little girl standing
under a tree waiting for someone. As the boy had
waited many years ago in my second song. At that
time, the male songwriters I studied and sought to em-
ulate wrote primarily from the man's point of view. So I
had tried to write a boy's story. Could it be the girl had
been waiting for the boy to arrive? No wonder I
couldn't solve the riddle of the lyric! If so, I was now

willing, eager to go out to meet her. It wouldn't be easy to enter her realm. She'd always been so shy, obediently silent, afraid to question or confide in anybody. Well, the moment I acknowledged her presence in my life it was like a floodgate opening. All the pent-up feelings poured out. She howled to have her say as she'd never been permitted by her parents, my parents, our parents. The child I used to be. In her voice, I wrote my childhood memoirs. The first ten years of Dorothy Langan's life I called "Midnight Baby." The child in me began to comprehend her environment. Our parents went through the same trip with their parents and theirs before them. She clearly saw the patterns with the unprejudiced mind of the child. And knew there is no blame.

After her book was completed I wrote four opening chapters as a contemporary introduction leading into the past, including the trip to the airport and the breakdown on the London-bound plane. Recalling, reliving that adult experience was a revelation, so many things began to fall into place. I already knew I'd been split into two people, the female side and the male side. But, in writing it out, I discovered when I went to the airport that day, *three* people got on the plane.

chapter 46

We're going to crash!
Kill the priest!
We're in danger!

Those were the "incoherent" accusations I'd hurled at
the stunned priest in my final attempt to fly. Eventually
I was able to piece together the mystery of those words.
On the way to the airport, a voice kept telling me to
push! Just as the woman had said in the hotel room
when I was seventeen. Push, Dorothy, push! But the
Los Angeles terminal was all confusion. I became
frightened of the crowds, my resolve began to melt.
Pull! Someone said. Just as my father used to say. You
can't get anywhere in this world without pull. And you
ain't got any pull, Dot, pull! Split in two, I again
reversed roles. I was being pushed ahead by the martyr
woman and pulled back by the crazy man. On the walls
of the terminal were some poster paintings of planes by
schoolchildren. The style of the drawings seemed familiar. Where had I seen them before? Suddenly, a
third person emerged from the confusion.

The child came forward, utterly convinced we were
being drawn on by the hands of Someone Unseen but
kind. In her eyes the airplane was safe as the child's
water color. Look, the front is smiling! The child cried
gleefully. See the letters on the side? Pan Am. Am
spelled backwards is Ma. And Pan spelled backward is

nap. We'll just go on board, take a nice nap in Ma's lap and we'll wake up safe and sound in London-town.

He! He! Now I know the reason for the giddy laugh. The child saw herself as pregnant with her first mother. I assumed she meant Florence, our mother. But no, she meant Dory. And Dory was two-headed. Actually the child was in full possession of both her parents. The child was carrying twins. The unnatural weightiness made her more giddily confident. Her (two-way) ticket was stamped. Her (matched) luggage checked. No (adult) anxieties. A child was in control and foolhardily free of panic. We hurried to the waiting room and looked out the window. The plane was smiling. See, said the child, I was right. We climbed into the belly of the plane and strapped ourselves into our seat. But—. What—? Never mind. What! The crazy voice demanded. Well, on the way in, I noticed. The initials. Yesss? Pan Am. PA. The initials spell Pa-Daddy-God-Father. They mean father! No, no, said the child. Not *mean*.father. *Grand* father. Our favorite. Patrick Shannon. But he's dead. Right. That's why he's coming back as Sidney Poitier. The clue is in the initials. S. P. is P. S. backwards. Sidney Poitier/Patrick Shannon. Get it? Oh, yes. I remember now. The empty seat next to mine is going to be taken by my own darling grandfather. Daddy always called Mama's papa black Irish. Sidney Poitier is just a disguise. He's really my *black Irish grandpa* who'll take me across the Atlantic to the home of our ancestors where we'll all live safely ever after. But where is he? Why doesn't he come? We looked anxiously toward the door and that's when we saw the priest.

He came down the aisle toward us. We grew alarmed. We thought the priest recognized me and would cry *killer.* Once found out, we'd be given a hurried penance and thrown out of the plane as his ancestor threw me out of the confessional. We were in danger. The screams were a deliberate, unconscious, desperate effort to be spirited away to the safety of an asylum. For the first time I felt no despair at being locked in. At last my tangled family was clearly divided. The man and woman had returned to their origins and found their child.

The confinement in the snake-pit among our fellow cuckoos would give us time, we three, ragged monstrous family, to go down into our swamp and consciously trot along after our child as she skipped after her lost soulmate. Then we would responsibly allow the soul-child to lead us back to our long forgotten center. Where we will see ourselves as very small. Small enough to sit under a limb of a fir tree. Silent enough to listen for our pulse as it tunes into the singer. Reflective enough for the Muse to project the message of the medium.

We will still keep a weather-beaten eye on space. We won't turn a deafened ear to the big-time pop-oracles. We will even try to tap-dance along behind the high, leaping, strut-swinging steps of the last beats of this twentieth century. (Sometimes, I feel the child in me is so involved in the past she's circled back around and stands in the future waiting for me to catch up.) But one has new defenses for the new age. Different choices. Other paths. Alternative patterns. There is a more organic pulse more softly insistant than the electronic pounding of the hard rock mountain. A phosphorescence that glows low within while the high of the neon tube burns itself out. There is a spherical singer to waltz round in time to when one feels considered by some to be square. I feel a deeper consideration of what we have here, now. In our place. Our planet is very solid substantial fare. Yet so fragile it dances on air. Could we be different? I doubt it.

> we are everything and nothing
> but that's how to play the game
> in these weather beaten bodies
> with these god forsaken brains
> we can listen
> listen
> listen to the universe resounding
> in the pulsing and the pounding
> of our infant ancient veins
> listen
> listen
> listen and it all begins to fit
> you are it
> you are it
> *we* are it. . . .

chapter 47

As for what *it* is, I haven't the vaguest idea. But whatever it is, we are of it. Possibly all life is simply that. Stuff of it. But this advanced technological, scientific, psychiatric world sometimes seems too complex to understand anything so simple. If I may paraphrase Groucho Marx, *It* is so simple a four-year-old child could understand it, so get me a four-year-old child! Get me one, too! For I am in danger of growing too rational and have much to learn from her soul. And to coin another cliché, what does it profit a woman if she gains the whole damned rational world and suffers the loss of her simple-minded child? Yes? Yes. Aha!

hello . . .

chapter 48

At last I am able to reply to the reflection in the deep inner stream. Down in the realm of the marsh. What I am is, a bog-trotter. Muddy-footed. Irish as Paddy's pig. And my rightful name is the same as the river by which my Mother was called. There is no more need for disguises. This time, I was not strong enough to pull aside the artificial lace curtain. But the next time, I will be. The next book will be written by Dory Shannon.

chapter 49

And yet. Had the writing of lyrics taken me too far? Trotting along the unpaved road I had aspired to the verse of nightingale and cultivated rosebud. Instead of angel song I found the cry of the crow. I began with an eye toward finding my one true mythical king who collaborated with a full moon that obediently rhymed with June and spoon. But my unbalanced craft drove me into the runcible reaches of my memory. Don't lose your soul, my father warned. Don't get hurt, my mother cried. I disobeyed both. My harmless tunes asswhipped me on a perilous journey from leprechauns and lambswool to demons and monsters. Then dumped me into the metaforest of my boggy-brain, in the dingy center of which lay the gill-gasping remains of a shoeless soul frog-croaking at the backside of the moon. No. I hadn't gone too far. I wish now to give media validation to this, too.

I am a freak. Fragmented as this book. A monstrous hydra-headed woman-man dwarf-soul girl-child. All dancing all singing all talking. A union of voices,

divided under my Muse. Less than the sum of my parts.
I am an attraction of opposites. Ain't that something.
Ain't that wild.

> the kind that grew
> in her grandmother's arbor
> when she was a child
> and the monster smiled
> roses red roses wild
> roses grateful
> the monster smiled.

Some Early Songs (1950s)

the girl

(fragment)

. . . the night
was growing cold
the moon
was getting dim
he sat there
growing old
at least
it seemed
that way to him
he waited
past forever
to keep his love alive
but
the girl
did not arrive.

leprechauns
are upon me

what is this
thing amiss
i'm elated
with unadulterated
bliss!

leprechauns
are upon me
pixies are playing tricks
i'm right in the middle

of cat and the fiddle
and hi-diddle-diddle-dee-dee!

a water sprite
delights me
elves are showing themselves
i'm laughin' and clappin'
i'm sure i am nappin'
how else could this happen to me?

i've found the key
to a world of glee
i'm seein'
everything clearer
the world is my palace
i feel just like alice
when she stepped
into the mirror!

leprechauns
are upon me
darned if
the moon isn't blue
for hi-diddle-diddle
you've answered the riddle
of whether you
love me too!

many sides

there are always
many sides
to a situation
and its hard
when any man
tries an explanation
but its harder yet
for a man to get
to know himself alone
for every man has
many sides
he has never even shown
many sides
that he himself
has never known . . .

we've a good side
and a bad side
we've a bright side
and a sad side
and the right hand
never knows
what the left
will do

we've a young side
and an old side
we've a kind side
and a cold side
and the mind
will never learn
how the heart
knows who

who is the one
the only one
for every part
for every heart
has cried
you can be satisfied
by a love that's tried
and true

true the sad side
to the bad side
to the glad side
true to you.

my heart is a hunter

what am i seeking
in the vast unknown
what am i seeking
all alone?

my heart is a hunter
it roams the night
leaving behind
the here and now

my heart is a hunter
it combs the sky
will it unwind
the why and how?

longingly gazing
at distance

wanting to learn
where it goes
the moon
in its lonely
existence
knows
but not i

my heart is a hunter
and vows to roam
till it will find
till it will find
a home.

yes

if he asks me
will i stay
and never go away
i'll tell him yes
i'll tell him yes

and if he should
hold me fast
and whisper will it last
i'll tell him yes
i'll tell him yes

yes
yes to every question
yes to ev'ry whim
i've no other answer
when it comes to him

unless
he happens
to suggest
perhaps it would be best
if he should go
if he should go
if he asks me
wouldn't it be
just as well
i'll tell him no
i'll tell him no.

like love

drop the politics
and pretensions
skip the subject
of new dimensions
let's begin about
your intentions
do you happen to
like love?

nothin' lower than
high type theories
bring 'em up
and i get the wearies
so the dodgers
will blow the series
do you happen to
like love?

i happen to love love
i happen to have
my mind on it
speak to me of love
and maybe you'll find
love is a thing
that is bigger than big
love is a thing
that you happen
to dig

take your lectures
and take your studies
give 'em back
to the fuddy-duddies
let's pretend
we're a pair of buddies
who just happen to
like love

i happen to love love
i happen to have
my mind on it
speak to me of love
and maybe you'll find
love is a treat
that you shouldn't avoid
might even beat
a discussion of freud

take your lectures
and goodly habits
give 'em back
to the squares and babbitts
let's pretend
we're a pair of rabbits
who just happen to
like love.

control yourself

control yourself
contain yourself
restrict yourself
restrain yourself
and always let
tranquility
be your goal

control yourself
contain yourself
and if you can't
explain yourself
and try to act
agreeably
on the whole

life is far too short
to spend it in a huff
try to be
the sort of guy
who laughs
when things get rough!

control yourself
contain yourself
you can and still
remain yourself
if you will let
serenity
in your soul
you must
contain yourself
restrain yourself

and train yourself
to gain your
self control!

just for now

love the leaves are falling
barren is the bough
so each descends
as autumn ends
not forever
just for now

love the earth is sleeping
silent 'neath the plow
so nothing grows
as winter snows
not forever
just for now

then spring arrives
to take the chill
to put fresh flowers
on the hill
to light the sun
and summer skies
that brightly burn
till summer dies

love the world keeps changing
time will not allow
this little night

to keep from flight
so let me show you
how to love me
not forever
i'd never ask for ever
to love me
not forever
just for now.

it's good to have you near again

it's good to have you
near again
it's pointless to disguise
how good it is to
hear again
your sweet familiar lies

it's good to have you say again
you're home forever more
you'll never go away again
as you have done before

anything you tell me
i'll believe
is true
though the only one
that you deceive
is you

the stories you have told
my love
could never be the truth

you're just a little old
my love
to blame it on your youth
but till you disappear again
i want it understood
to have you near again
is good.

change of heart

your face i remember
your walk is the same
the voice is familiar
so is the name
you're all i adore
but you're not as before
you've had a change of heart

it's not that you're different
you're just as you were
why you're even wearing
the tie i prefer
it's nothing that shows
yet the certainty grows
you've had a change of heart

now that i notice
your smile's not at ease
your laugh isn't nearly
as eager to please
your phrases are tender
to no avail
your eyes tell another tale

oh yes i remember
i love ev'ry part
your face and your voice
but it's foolish to start
for the more i reveal
the less you conceal
you've had a change of heart.

Some Film Songs

the faraway part of town

lonely
she roamed through the city
the buildings
seemed barren and brown
she was lost in the lights
of the distance
in the faraway part of town

faraway faraway
might just as well be a
star away
over there
where she longed to be
when would she go
what would she see?

slowly
she walked and she wondered
the river
reflected her frown
she was certain that someone was waiting
in the faraway part of town

faraway faraway
how many strangers there
are away
over there
where she longed to run
how would she know
who was the one?
the faraway heart
the faraway heart
in the faraway part
of town.
    (from *Pepe*)

a second chance

can't i have
a second chance
i won't ask for any more
can't you give
a second chance
when you've had three or four
perhaps you couldn't
tell it was love
well, it was love with me
but now it's turn-about
i'm out
does it have to be?

can't i have
a second chance
it's so little to demand
won't you take
a second chance
then you might understand
you're more than just an
end of the road
friend of the road
with me
you're my first
my one romance
can't i have
a second chance?

[from *Two for the Seesaw*]

goodbye charlie

goodbye charlie
hate to see you go
goodbye charlie
gee i'm feelin' low
but i'm cluein' you in
someone's doin' you in pal

goodbye charlie
hate to see you fade
my my charlie
thought you had it made
but they're dumpin' you off
after bumpin' you off pal

don't you know lechery
leads you to treachery
things boomerang
someone you trifle with
pulls out a rifle without a pang
bang bang bang

goodbye charlie
cashin' in your chips
goodbye charlie
time you came to grips
there ain't no doubt
strike three you're out
goodbye charlie
goodbye.

[from *Goodbye Charlie*]

your smile

i heard you speak
i touched your cheek
and then i saw your smile
much more than grand
i held your hand
and then i saw your smile

a fleeting thing
a rose in spring
it bloomed
for just a while

on that wond'rous place
your wond'rous face
i was filled with awe
when i saw
your smile.

[from *Who Was That Lady?*]

you're gonna hear from me

everyone tells me
to know my place
but that ain't
the way i play
why am i daring

to show my face?
'cause i've got
something to say!

move over sun
and give me some sky
i've got me some wings
i'm eager to try
i may be unknown
but wait till i've flown
you're gonna hear from me

make me some room
you people up there
on top of the world
i'll meet you i swear
i'm staking my claim
remember my name
you're gonna hear from me

fortune smiled
on the road before me
i'm fortune's child
listen world
you can't ignore me

i've got a song
that longs to be played
raise up my flag
begin my parade
then watch the world over
start coming up clover
that's how it's gonna be
you'll see
you're gonna hear from me!

   [from *Inside Daisy Clover*]

theme

gotta get off
gonna get
have to get off
from this ride
gotta get hold
gonna get
need to get hold
of my pride

when did i get
where did i
how was i caught
in this game
when will i know
where will i
how will i
think of my name

when did i stop
feeling sure
feeling safe
and start wondering why
wondering why
is this a dream
am i here
where are you
what's in back of the sky
why do we cry?

gotta get off
gonna get
outa this
merry-go-round

gotta get on
gonna get
need to get
on where i'm bound
when did i get
where did i
why am i
lost as a lamb
when will i know
where will i
how will i learn
who i am

is this a dream
am i here
where are you
tell me
when will i know
how will i know
when will i know
why?

[from *Valley of the Dolls*]

i'll plant my own tree

i'll plant my own tree
and i'll make it grow
my tree
will not be
just one in a row

my tree
will offer shade
when strangers go by
if you're a stranger
brother
well so am i

come tomorrow
all that i see
is my tree
oh lord what a sight
let someone stop me
and i will put up a fight

it's my yard
so i will try hard
to welcome friends
i've yet to know
oh i'll plant my own tree
my own tree
and i'll make it
grow!

[from *Valley of the Dolls*]

say goodbye

when i was a babe
the sea and the sun
were the mother's arms
to which i'd run
secure
beneath the pure
maternal sky
time went on
we grew apart
and i forgot
my mother's heart
a heart deprived of love
can only cry
and i am
going away
i heard her say
i'm going away
i heard her say
i'm going away
won't someone say goodbye?

when i was a child
i ruled the earth
i owned it all
its total worth
each fish each field
each flower each butterfly
then one day
it occurred to me
if i own the earth
then the earth owns me
and each of us must live
or both of us will die

and i am
going away
i heard her say
i'm going away
i heard her say
i'm going away
won't someone say goodbye?

alone in space
we together float
a frightened crew
in a fragile boat
and each of us must live
or both will die
each of us must live
or both will die
and i am
going away
i heard her say
i'm going away
i heard her say
i'm going away
won't someone say goodbye?

[from *Say Goodbye*]

come saturday morning

come saturday morning
i'm going away
with my friend
we'll saturday spend
till the end of the day
just i and my friend
we'll travel for miles
in our saturday smiles
then
we'll move on
but we will remember
long after saturday's
gone.
  [from *The Sterile Cuckoo*]

last tango in paris

we don't exist
we are nothing
but shadow and mist
in the mirror
we look as we pass
no reflection's revealed
in the glass

don't you know
that the blood in your vein
is as lifeless as
yesterday's rain?

it's a game
where we come
to conceal
the confusion we feel
but long as we're nameless
our bodies are blameless

you cried
when we kissed
it was nothing
but shadow and mist
two illusions
who touch in a trance
making love
not by choice
but by chance

to a tune
that we tore from the past
to a tango we swore
was the last
we are shadows who dance
we are shadows who dance
we are shadows who dance. . . .

    [from *Last Tango in Paris*]

should i call you mister?

should i call you mister
should i call you sir
should i be a sister
which would you prefer
what if there's another
should i then pretend
you are just a brother
could i call you friend?

should i call you lover
would you disagree
would you then discover
what you mean to me
brother friend and lover
everything that's fine
please may i call you mine?

[from *Goodbye, Mr. Chips*
unproduced, circa 1962]

goodbye

goodbye goodbye
no time for tears
no time to wonder why
goodbye reply
my younger years
yet i can scarcely sigh

goodbye goodbye
i've no regret
i lost it on the way
with all the things
i'll never get
how small they seem today

goodbye to the book
i didn't write
goodbye to my silent song
farewell to the fears
i didn't fight
who's to say i was wrong?

goodbye goodbye
to dreams untold
i can't regret
they're through
goodbye goodbye
to something old
hello to something new
goodbye goodbye
to something old
hello
my love
to you.

[from *Goodbye, Mr. Chips*]

my boys

actually
i'd admit this to no one
no one but me perhaps
but when it comes down to cases
i'm attached to those little chaps
yet in a manner consistent
i would of course have to say
my relations with them are
well distant
and frankly
i like it that way

some are outgoing
some introspective
some are uncertain
of goals or objective
some of them freckled and dappled
cheeks either tanned or they're appled
some of them plod
some are so odd
some make such ear-splitting noise
some of them sturdy
most of them dirty
but bless them
they're all my boys

some are respectful
some are religious
some of their knowledge
of girls is prodigious
either they're saints or satanic
either they plague or they panic
some are so neat
some of them cheat

some have such unnerving poise
some strike such poses
none blow their noses
but bless them
they're all my boys

true our encounter is brief
they're only mine to borrow
and each with unspoken relief
leaves me some sudden tomorrow
i'm glad our relations are thin
they never get under my skin
i'm relieved when i see them all go
i'm quite unaffected
although
some seem so homesick
so sympathetic
some so Byronic'ly pale and poetic
what good am i but to teach them
yet how i wish i could reach them
but why should i care
it's not my affair
if some are too stout
and some broken out
if some have been dismal
since their baptismal
if some tend to cling to their toys

well i must admit
i care quite a bit
and while they are mine
they're my joys
they're my battles
they're my blessings
they're my boys.

[from *Goodbye, Mr. Chips*]

this time

this time
you can do it
this time
you'll come through
this time
you can take the world by the tail
listen now that you're older
you'll be better and bolder
speaking straight
from the shoulder
you aren't going to fail
it's easy sailing for you

this time
something's in you
this time
you can win
last time
there was something
made you afraid
not that you were a coward
you just felt over-powered
but you suddenly flowered
and you can make the grade
you'll be parading
with the ones up there
with the confident air
who demand their share
of the show

this time
you can do it
this time
you'll come through it

this time
i know!

this time
is the right time
this time
he can fight
this time
he can face the world all alone
there is nothing can beat him
they will see when they meet him
who would dare to defeat him
now that he's on his own
there's no postponing for him

this time
he'll surprise them
this time
he'll be wise
last time
he was simply lost in the mob
when a man is neglected
it can make him dejected
but that's all been corrected
and he can do the job
he'll be hobnobbing
with that special breed
who are bound to succeed
and his ev'ry deed
will endure

this time
he can do it
this time
he'll come through it
this time
i'm sure!

[from *Goodbye, Mr. Chips*]

empty is my room

the wind
is a cruel companion
whistling at the gloom
beneath the door
across the floor
empty is my room

a star
with a fixed expression
calmly stares at strife
its look is brief
upon our grief
empty is my life

i'll dwell
in time remembered
my home
ever far away
i'll hold
the child i never held
in a place
called yesterday

if not
i must cry to Katherine,
why did you depart
and take your bloom
from my life and my room
and leave
my empty heart?

    [from *Goodbye, Mr. Chips*]

they're going nowhere

they're going nowhere
their dreams are packed
but going nowhere
and that's a fact
their hearts are ready
their hopes are high
but going nowhere
their lives a lie

how can they
delude themselves
how can they
include themselves
in that group who climb the peak
ride the river to what they seek
they're wonderful fools
but they're weak
they're weak

they're going nowhere
their feet are still
it hasn't happened
it never will
they're full of promise
and grand goodbye
but going nowhere
the same as i

is it
i'm content to be
is it
i am meant to be
in that group who stand and stare
never daring to cross the square

those pitiful fools
who are there
just there

just doing nothing
forever bound
to run in circles
around and round
they're going nowhere
the same as i
i must go somewhere
i must
or die!
   [from *Thieves' Carnival*
   unproduced, circa 1964]

heaven only knows

tell me what is real
tell me what is not
oftentimes i worry
and i wonder
what is what
breezes brush my face
yet they can't be seen
heaven only knows
if the grass
is really green

what is there to be
what is there to come
are we simply headed
for the place

we're coming from
if we move along
while we spin around
heaven only knows
if our feet
are on the ground

when are we awake
when we are asleep
are the dreams
we think we've lost
the ones we really keep
time continues on
tell me where
it goes
heaven only knows
if a rose
is just a rose

where the river flows
why a person grows
will we ever learn
do you suppose
all the things
that
heaven only knows?

[from *Thieves' Carnival*]

here am i

friendless star
endless sky
heartless as a stone
when will we discover
what we should have known
borrowed time
borrowed place
everything on loan
in this temporary world
love is all we own
in this temporary world
love is all we own. . .

here am i
within this time
within this place
within this night
beneath that sky
here am i

here are you
within these walls
within this world
within this space
beneath that star
here you are

friendless star
endless sky
careless of our plight
love is all that listens
when we call
within the night
yet we hide

within our pride
wordless as we cry
if i could say
i need you
if you would only try

you could be
within my arms
within my heart
within my life
beneath that vast unknown
but nothing's said
we stand instead
within ourselves alone.

[from *Thieves' Carnival*]

to find myself

to find myself
to find myself
i'm going out of
my mind myself
what myself
who myself
introduce me
to myself
what am i
who am i
what am i to do?

to find myself
to find myself
what a fruitless chase

since i've never seen myself
or met me face to face
i'm sure i'm someone special
never trite or small
the way i see myself
is not what others see at all
i know i must be handsome
someone great and grand
i sure would like
to find myself
so i could shake my hand!

what a task
to find myself
i don't like to boast
but i'm so well-disguised
by now i fool myself the most
i'm sure there's someone special
i have covered up
that someone in my looking glass
who stirs my shaving cup
of course i'm someone handsome
someone big with tips
if i could ever find myself
i'd kiss me on the lips!

to find myself
to find myself
am i in front or
behind myself
where myself
show myself
i'll never get to
know myself
where am i
who am i
what am i to do?

to find myself
to find myself
where's the fun in that
what's the sense in searching
when i don't know where i'm at
am i up the river
am i down the street
am i out there sitting
in a third row center seat
am i just an actor
playing in a part
i'd never be an actor,
no, for that i'm much too smart!

what a task
to find myself
who am i to call
suppose i find myself
and i don't like myself at all?
suppose that when i find me
and penetrate my shell
i find i'm less than nothing
in fact
i look like hell!
suppose i'm no one handsome
no one brave and strong
how could i have
believed myself
deceived myself
so long?

to find myself
to find myself
how could i have been
so blind myself
where myself
what myself

forgive me i am
not myself
what am i
who am i
what am i to do. . .

to find myself
to find myself
what a fruitless chase
since i've never seen myself
or met me face to face
i *think* i'm someone special
never trite or small
the way i see myself
is *not* what others see at all
i *must* be someone handsome
i *know* i'm brave and strong

i'm *sure* i'm someone special
and i am never wrong
about myself
about myself
i've not the slightest
doubt myself
good myself
kind myself
that is how
i find myself
strong myself brave myself
long may i wave myself
me myself
free myself
let me be
be myself
i myself and me!

    [from *Thieves' Carnival*]

in early morn

in early morn
when day was born
i dressed in simple taste
unadorned
the gown i chose
except for a rose
a pale pale rose
pinned to my tiny waist my dear
pinned to my tiny waist

as day passed on
with morning gone
i added something more
something new
in brighter blue
along with the rose
a pearl or two
pinned to the dress i wore that year
pinned to the dress i wore

in the swift
descending shade
rose and pearl
began to fade
so i added to my sash
blazing rubies
flashing jade
sparkling diamonds
brilliant white
capture a sunbeam
just as the day
takes flight
and the later it grows
the more i seem

to feel the need
to glitter and gleam
but its harder
to keep it light and clear
its harder to keep it light

my jewels spark
as day grows dark
my dress is blinding bright
all ablaze
at night's approach
(in place of the rose
a sapphire brooch)
diamond sparkle
emerald earring
keep the day
from disappearing
still
it will soon be night i fear
still
it will soon be night.

[from *Thieves' Carnival*]

the old soft sell
(a soft shoe)

tell 'em they're great
make with the punch
soon you'll become
one of the bunch
tell 'em a joke
give 'em a poke
ring in yourself like a bell
give 'em the old soft sell!

butter 'em up
spread yourself thin
what do you care
long as you're in
show 'em your style
throw 'em a smile
howl at the stories they tell
give 'em the old soft sell!

in these modern days y'know
advertising pays y'know
smirkery does it
or smuggerery does it
but always remember
skullduggery does it
talk in big amounts y'know
it's what's up front that counts y'know
up the vote does it
and down the vote does it
but always remember
that down the throat does it!

tell 'em they're swell
rub it in well

spread it on thick
till they get sick
tell them that we
are g-r-a-t
assuming of course they can spell
give 'em the old soft sell!

promise the moon
what do you care
throw 'em a bone
then throw 'em a scare
first you're a pest
next you're a guest
then when they start to rebel
give 'em the old soft sell!

if they get bored
don't let it lag
snap 'em in step
raise up a flag
make 'em salute
get 'em to root
then when they holler and yell
give 'em the old soft sell

in these modern days y'know
advertising pays y'know
actively does it
or verbally does it
but always remember
hyperbole does it
get yourself a jingle boys
make their senses tingle boys
live it up does it
and love it up does it
but always remember
that shove it up does it!

shoot off your mouth
listen to none
can't get their ears?
shoot off a gun!
the bigger the lie
the bigger they buy
hang in the air like a smell
give 'em the old soft sell
give 'em the old soft
and if you find
that you're losin' the jerks
always remember
that dynamite works
while you're givin' 'em hell
give 'em the old soft sell
POW!

[from *Thieves' Carnival*]

Some Other Songs (1960s–70s)

down the drain

i washed a baby
down the drain
it was a baby
it couldn't complain
it disappeared
in the red tinted water
i never knew
was it a son
or a daughter?

i washed a baby
down the drain
it was a baby
it couldn't complain
when i confessed
to the parish priest
he hated me
but he forgave me
at least

modest in his
woman-skirt
revolted by my
woman-hurt
sweat and tears
and cursing pain
life is lost
and found insane
tell the nun
to run
for holy water
from the bowl
i've smeared
his spotless soul

with
woman-dirt

i washed a baby
down the drain
it was a baby
it couldn't complain
a stain or two
on the sheets of a bed
that's all that's left
'cept for my head
don't sprinkle holy water on
the mark of cain
just let me stand awhile
in the rain. . . .

so long mom
so long dad

so long mom
so long dad
i just got married
but don't feel bad
you won't have to tell me
'bout the birds and bees
'cause for quite a few years
i've done as i please
and we're going out
to los angeles
where the oranges
grow on trees

i hate to fly
in an aeroplane
so we're gonna take
the choo-choo train

the endless trip
they say is worth
the chance to ball
in an upper berth

so long mom
so long dad
got something to tell you
but don't be mad
i married a guy
the two of you
used to describe as
a typical jew
i'm sorry
folks
he ain't our kind
but i don't think
jesus will mind

jesus' name was
emmanuel
he was a nice jewish boy
so what the hell
if he could stand it
well so can you
besides there's nothing
that you can do

so long mom
so long dad
i just got married
but don't feel bad
'cause we're going out
to los angeles
where the oranges
grow on trees
the oranges
grow on trees.

men wander
women weep

men wander
women weep
women worry
while men are asleep
men wander
while women weep
and that's the way
it goes

i waited for you love
all last night
i listened to music
and kept on the light
i watched the morning
and walked the floor
till i heard your key
in my open door

men wander
women weep
women worry
while men are asleep
men wander
while women weep
and that's the way
it goes

as soon as i thought love
i heard your key
i put out the light love
so you wouldn't see
i shut off the music
and faced the wall

but it wasn't your key
i'd heard at all

men wander
women weep
women worry
while men are asleep
men wander
while women weep
and that's the way
it goes

tonight i am certain
i'll wait some more
till i hear your footstep
at my front door
if you don't show up love
i'll curse all men
and tomorrow night
i'll be waitin' again

men wander
women weep
women worry
while men are asleep
men wander
while women weep
and that's the way
it goes

love with women
is very deep
love with men
is a thing
that can keep
they won't admit it
but ev'ry woman knows
that's the way
it goes.

for Claudia Previn & Alicia Previn

two daughters

he has two daughters
two slender daughters
one is apricot fair
one has daffodil hair
one's heart is brave
one's eyes are very grave
and grey

he has two daughters
two tender daughters
one is quiet and just
one has innocence and trust
one bares a scar
one learned on my guitar
to play

the younger rides a pony
a wild and roving kind
the other has her books
and travels only in her mind
beautiful are they
beautiful are they

he has two daughters
two splendid daughters
since he left on a whim
they'll remind me of him
they have his look
his laugh the love he took
away
his reflection flows

clear as crystal waters
through his two daughters
two slender daughters.

the house is him

every room
every wall
in the house i possess
is as empty as letters
that bear my address
the surroundings are mine
but never the less
the house is him

every mark
every grain
in the wood of the door
every thread in the carpet
that covers the floor
on the surface its me
but deep at the core
the house is him

so i must go
or constantly strive
to keep his sweet image
awake and alive
goodbye to halls
that echo his talk
goodbye to his whistle
as he comes up the walk
i will never forget him
i don't want to forget him

he is in
every mirror
pictures we took
he lives in each line
on each page of each book
he is there where i touch
i taste and i look
the house is him

every room
every wall
in the house i possess
is as empty as letters
that bear my address
he is here
he is there
he will never grow dim
the house is him.

i got a cat named cluny brown

i got a cat named cluny brown
she's my onliest friend in town
the world has cancelled out on me
but cluny loves me
yessirree
yessirree
yessirree

i got a cat named cluny brown
all she needs is a little ground round
a bowl of water and a pillow bed
and cluny loves me
when she's fed

when she's fed
when she's fed

cluny's weird
cluny's wise
velvet paws
jelly bean eyes
knows i'm lonely
knows i'm lazy
doesn't care
that i'm half crazy
and when i act
a stupid fool
she accepts me
cluny's cool

i got a cat named cluny brown
she's my up when i am down
when my true love went away
cluny settled
here to stay
here to stay
here to stay

i got a cat named cluny brown
she's my onliest friend in town
i'll never be rich
i'll never have fame
but cluny loves me
just the same
just the same
cluny loves me
just the same.

hair

hair
i love my hair
it isn't fair
how i love my hair
it's ten inches long
it's three inches thick
i comb it and spray it
and i get such a kick

hair
i love my hair
i really care
for my swingin' hair
whenever i jerk
it's somethin' to see
my sister's so jealous
that she wishes she was me

hair
i love my hair
it's hard to bear
how i love my hair
i go every day
for a set and shampoo
and the thing that's so great is
that my girl loves it too.

for Nikolas Venet

nikolas venetoulis
never should have
changed his name

nikolas venetoulis
never should have
changed his name
nikolas venetoulis
never should have played that game
you tell me
don't it put
your soul to shame?

nikolas venetoulis
never should have left that morn
he didn't have to turn his back on
the town where he was born
nikolas venetoulis
left his hometown
in the rain
you tell me
don't it make you feel forlorn?

he took his mother's
passport photo
with him
he took his grandpa's
amber worry beads
but he left
his father's name
behind him
at the bottom
of some faded mortgage deeds

he took a bottle
from the ketchup factory
to remind him
of the roots
he aimed to lose
he took his older brother's
only jacket
he took his younger brother's
sunday shoes

he ran away
from chains of church and childhood
sure that he'd
been born
a diff'rent breed
but the lettered name
across his father's mailbox
was the only thing
he ever came to need

some things
should be left unaltered
some things
must forever stay the same
nikolas
kostantinos
venetoulis
never should have
changed his name.

three-dollar room

why do i long
to take over the cross
what in the world
would be gained or be lost
why do i want
to replace sweet sufferin' jesus
who'd wake up and weep
the guests need their sleep

why do i feel
the need for to bleed
to do myself in
with the torturous deed
who down the hall
would be glad to be stuck
with the mess that remains
the desk clerk complains

why do i choose
to check out
unsuspected
some night in a
three-dollar room
no little white churches
were ever erected
for unwanted martyrs
(every three-dollar tomb
has color tv
included free)
nailed to the sheet
on a three-dollar bed
ain't no resurrectin'
the three-dollar dead
no refund allowed

for leaving too soon
says on the door
paid up till noon

yet i would dare
to bear my own blame
stealing from jesus
his sufferin' fame
why do i ask
to carry my luggage
pay my own bill
and leave when i will
some night in a
three-dollar room
let me atone
for nobody's sins
but my own.

for sylvia
who killed herself
in 1963

i have been
where sylvia's been
she did not survive
i came back
from where she was
i'm still
half alive

i saw all
that sylvia saw
both our minds
were burned

she went closer
to the sun
she did not
return

sylvia soared
on wings of fear
i flew too
but not so far
sylvia strayed
sylvia stayed
too long
sylvia shaped
and sculpted poems
from the granite
of a star
all that i
could do was try
to carve a simple song

her light
was bright as
seraphim
my candlewick
was dim
yet we both felt
our spirits melt
'neath sun
without a scrim

i envied sylvia
ariel eyed
and one of us
one of us
died.

be careful baby

be careful baby
be careful
use caution at what you see
if i look unsure or act insecure
that's the most dangerous part of me
you're not dealing now
with no mere winner
someone who's never learned
how it feels to take a fall
you're dealing in me with a loser
that's the strongest opponent of all
so be careful baby
be careful
which words and what weapons you choose
beware of tangling with underdogs
with someone
who's got nothing to lose

there is nothing
i got left on this earth
that's worth saving
my soul my self
my vanity my sanity
my god my lord
my precious virginity
i lost to a student of divinity
one ludicrous night
in the back seat
of a second-hand ford
(kick a person when she's up
and you can break her spirit you know
but kick a person when she's down
and all you break is your toe)

there is nothing
i haven't done or encountered
on my dauntless desperate downhill trip
i swallowed pride
i swallowed opinions
i swallowed pollution
i swallowed pills
i lost my license
i lost my luggage
and i lost my grip!

so be careful baby
be careful
cause i'll survive in spite of you
i'll survive in spite of me
which is a much harder thing to do
and hey someday
when you're no longer a winner
and you've burnt your tongue
on the taste of defeat
perhaps the day will come again
in another time
in another life
when the two of us will meet
and then you'll descend
to my level
and we'll lie side by side
in the dirt
and you'll expose your scars to me
and we'll agree
how it feels to be hurt
and after you've shown me your bruises
and your heart that beats lost
abandoned and wrecked
i will bow to my equal
and then
i will show you respect!

moon rock

it has been said
that a rock
might have been the very first weapon
not a broken branch
or a bone
but a rock
a rock
a rock alone
this is not definitely known
for i believe
that a rock
might have been the very first gift
not a flower
or a tiger tooth
but a rock
a rock
a rock in truth
weapon or gift
enemy or friend
how a world begins
is how a world will end

sing glory to the golf balls
that were driven across her breast
she was a very gracious hostess
to a most
a most ungrateful guest
he thanked his friends in houston town
he thanked his fellow mates
he thanked his god in his heaven above
and then he thanked his chief of state
his gratitude to mankind
was eloquent and plain

but he never thanked the lady
who allowed him in her domain
sing glory to the golf balls
that were driven across her breast
she was a very gracious hostess
to a most
a most ungrateful guest

was there some ancient astronaut
who landed on this earth
did he thank
this beautiful prehistoric planet
did he let her know her worth
and did some ancient embryo
watch what the astronaut did
'cause the way you treat the old lady
is the lesson
that you teach the kid
did the ancient astronaut
just before the lift
take a souvenir
like a weapon
or did he receive it
like a gift?

it has been said
that a rock
might have been the very first weapon
not a broken branch
or a bone
but a rock
a rock alone
weapon or gift
enemy or friend
how a world begins
is how our world will end.

Schiz phrenos

don't make waves

when i was a child
she taught me how
to turn the other cheek
never start a row she said
know when you shouldn't speak
listen dorothy
do be good
an obedient child behaves
bury your frown
down under the ground
and above all
don't make waves
that's how my mama
brought me up
and my mama gave me
good advice
here i am
i'm standing right here
didn't i turn out nice?

when i was a child
i sat so still
in my daddy's wicker chair
when company came
i was so good
they never knew i was there
listen dorothy
don't talk back
an obedient child behaves
bury your frown
down under the ground
and above all
don't make waves

that's how my mama
brought me up
and my mama gave me
good advice
here i am
i'm sitting right here
didn't i turn out nice?

when i was a child
i dutifully learned
to turn the other cheek
i swallowed my opinions whole
i knew when not to speak
now here i lie
beneath this stone
in one of the quieter graves
where my epitaph is carved:
she never did make waves
that's how my mama
brought me up
and my mama gave me
good advice
here i am
i'm lying right here
didn't i turn out nice?

aunt rose
and the blessed event

daddy boarded up
the dining room
and locked us in
we three
four and a half months
we lived in that room
my mama the baby and me
my mama slept on the table
i slept on a cot
the baby was in a basket
i hated it a lot

we'd listen
till he went off to work
then we'd sneak out
for eggs
i'd run around the kitchen
to stretch my stumpy legs
we'd finish our eggs and coffee
then we'd make it neat
so daddy wouldn't go all crazy
'cause we came out to eat

one monday
after christmas day
he let my mama free
the week after that
i came out
the baby
he still wouldn't see
at night we'd go back in there
the reason i forgot

the baby didn't know the diff'rence
i hated it a lot

aunt rose came by
to visit us
bring out the kid
she said
mama says
godinhisgoodnessno
that man would shoot me dead
my mama says
he ain't seen it yet
her face went white as pearl
he don't know if the kid i had
is a boy or a little girl

well
aunt rose brought out
the baby
and laid it in the light of the tree
daddy arrived home
early from the job
and pretended
like he didn't see

so rosie picked up
the baby
and shoved it at him
on the spot
i watched him
take my sister
i hated it a lot

from then on
we were a family
we even had some fun
the boards
on the dining room door

came down
and daddy put away his gun
and
i forgot it happened
like something
i'd been dreaming
till eighteen odd years later
when i suddenly woke up
screaming.

i was you baby

i smiled
your smile
till my mouth
was set
and my face
was tight
and it wasn't right
it was wrong
i was you baby
i was you too long

i said
your words
till my throat
closed up
and i had
no voice
and i had
no choice
but to do your song

i was you baby
i was you too long

i lived
your life
till there was
no me
i was flesh
i was hair
but i wasn't there
it was wrong
i was you baby
i was you too long
and baby baby
the worst thing
to it
is that you let me
do it
so who was weak
and who was strong
for too long baby
i was you.

for five years
i was terrified
to get on a plane

i think i could have made it
but you killed me with conditions
just one suitcase
just one week
your own hotel

i can't meet you at the airport
i'll send someone out to get you
don't come monday
wait till tuesday
call me
swell

you can come to my rehearsals
but i'm busy on the weekend
i'll come any
way i love you
yes
but well

god i can't believe you're coming
i know isn't it fantastic
are you happy
wait till tuesday
go
to
hell.

common sense, circa '35

why don't you leave him mama
how come you take it like that
boy mama if you had any sense
you'd walk out
and leave him flat

when i am big
no man will do
what daddy went
and did to you

i thought of this
that whole night long
how did mama
get so wrong?

common sense, circa '69

why don't you leave him dory
how come you take it like that
boy dory is you had any sense
you'd walk out
and leave him flat

but who's got sense
my mama cried
tucking me in
in 'thirty-five

now i am big
and recall that night
how did mama
get so right?

two planes cracked up

two planes cracked up
and fell into the L.A. sea
two planes cracked up
my mama said
things come in three
then i cracked up in L.A.
i cracked up in L.A.
i cracked up in L.A.
and no one felt
the crash but me

my plane was two hours late
we waited on the strip
we never left the runway
but i went on a trip
on a trip
on a trip

two planes cracked up
the week before i damned near flew
two planes cracked up
so i did what i had to do
forgive me pan am airlines
forgive me pan am airlines
forgive me pan am airlines
for taking off
but not with you.

two a.m. with a guard

it's two a.m.
i cannot sleep
i pace the halls
someone is calling
help me hey someone help me
i guess it beats counting sheep
i know it beats counting sheep

it's two fifteen
i sit in fear
i have a guard
someone is sobbing
i love you yes no i don't
i guess the guard doesn't hear
i know the guard doesn't hear

it's three a.m.
someone just screamed
i stand aloof
and listen to the torment
jesus jesus jesus
i guess it's something someone dreamed
it must be something someone dreamed

i head for my room
well don't you see
i'd get some sleep
if they'd stop
calling cursing crying
if all those voices
would let me be
let me be
at two a.m.
when no one is awake
but me.

visitor's hour

judy and don
came to see me
the technician undid the lock
i showed them
the inner attractions
the meds
the straps
the shock

nervously
don admitted
sensing danger of a kind
like someone might
hide in a doorway
and hit
him from
behind

i laughed
and reassured him
the techs are always on guard
one sign
of a patient's violence
they move in
hard

but
i had seen
a face in a doorway
i recalled when they had gone
a boy hid
behind don's shoulder
the boy
i'd seen
was don.

watching the fish in the tank
for therapy

black molly
swims with her own reflection
is she mirrored in the sky
or in the iris of an eye

black molly
flirts with her rear projection
her own image is her guide
once her body's satisfied

watch her ball
with her brother
full of fertility food
who'll take the kids
from the mother
when she delivers her brood

black molly
caught by her own complexion
altogether self involved
molly o
your problem's solved

when you're full
you drop your dung
when you're empty
you eat your young.

let's play

don't be such a baby
act like a nice big girl
if you weren't such a baby
you wouldn't need to curl
into that position
who're you trying to test
we're gonna give you something girl
so you can get some rest

don't be such a baby
man the trick she tried
with both feet in the toilet
she forced herself inside
then she turned the handle
i guess it wouldn't flush
we found her on the bathroom floor
don't be a baby hush

what is that you're humming
tell it to the guard
catatonia
catatonia
what makes my big head so hard?

e.s.t.

please doc
don't let them
give me shock
i ask you
don't blow my mind
with a block

please doc
keep me back here
in the lock
i tell you
i don't want it done
with shock

e.s.t.
e.s.t.
they go in crying
and they come out whee!
the temple's burnt
the jawbone's tense
they feel just great
but they make no sense

please doc
don't break my
brain with a rock
i warn you
i won't let them
give me shock

when i am
on a downward swing
and cry:
i'll try anything

just make it stop!
don't listen to me doc
don't give me shock.

gotta stop depending

gotta stop depending
on those devils
gotta get my surface
neat and straight
why can't i just do it
lord i miss the trees
may i have a tranquilizer please?

gotta learn to face
the competition
everybody's scared
the same as me
wonder what they're thinking
something that i said
may i have two more to mend my head?

you sure i got no letter?
christ
these california showers
may i have a pill
to get some sleep?
all i need's a couple of hours
how come no one sends me flowers?

gotta stop pretending
i'm adjusted
screw them all

and let the surface crack
may i be psychotic?
please may i trip out?
may i be?
i mean
what i'm about?
may i?
may i?
may i?

i can't go on

i can't go on
i mean
i can't go on
i really
can't go on
i swear
i can't go on

so
i guess
i'll get up
and go on.

broken soul
  (schiz: broken
  phrenos: soul)

if i could take you love
on a voyage
from outer to inner
from a sort of life
to a kind of death
beyond heartbeat
beyond breath
beyond back
if i could take you there
(i have been you know)
would you come with me?
have you courage to go?

if i could lead you love
on a voyage
from here now
to no now
from the selfish time
to the timeless self
behind demons
behind beginnings
behind light
if i could take you there
oh the things you'd see
you may lose your way
of course
there is no guarantee

you will become entangled
in the simultaneous vision
of sea floors
and far stars

one eye pointed up and out
the other pointed down and in
and your
self
groping stunned and unbalanced
between the two
you will break your soul
be sure
broken soul
broken defenses
lose your mind
come to your senses

if i could take you love
then return you
from inner to inner/outer
from the eternal womb
through a second birth
into then now
with all you in you
split into one
if i could take you there
if you would explore
if i could tell you love
                    there is more.

listen

i no longer plead with heaven
or go rummaging in books
for answers to the questions
life contains
now i listen
listen
listen to this inner thing resounding
in the pulsing and the pounding
of my infant ancient veins

i no longer seek instruction
from my father and my mother
i have mastered
all their pleasures and their pain
no i listen
listen
listen to this inner thing resounding
in the pulsing and the pounding
of my infant ancient veins

the feeling in my bloodflow
is a simple thing y'see
everything and nothing
in the parody is me
i'm the hero
i'm the villain
the beginning and the end
i'm creator
i'm destroyer
i'm the enemy the friend
i'm an animal
a spirit
flying high and falling down

i am special
i'm important
i am sacred
i'm a clown
so i stumble through the chaos
dragging clumsily behind me
all the eggshells
and the fish scales
and the fur pelts of my past
while this thing goes on
inside me at one with all
the vastness
the fantasies
and fictions
and when all the contradictions
come together
come together
they will fit

the feeling in my bloodflow
is a simple thing y'see
i am it
i am it
we are everything and nothing
but that's how to play the game
in these weather-beaten bodies
with these god forsaken brains
we can listen
listen
listen to the universe resounding
in the pulsing and the pounding
of our infant ancient veins
listen
listen
listen and it all begins to fit
you are it
you are it

On My Way To Where (1968–69)

scared to be alone

we never stop to wonder
till a person's gone
we never yearn
to know him
till he's traveled on
when someone is around us
we never stop to ask
hey what's behind your mirror
hey who's beneath your mask
we never stop to wonder
till a person's gone
we never yearn
to know him
till he's packed
and traveled on

sweet marilyn monroe
on the silver screen
platinum reflection
in a movie magazine
well did you ever
have a headache
did your mama own a gramophone
did you like to be an actress
were you scared
to be alone?

we never stop to wonder
till a person's gone
we never yearn
to know him
till he's traveled on
when someone is around us
we don't know what we're seeing

we take a polaroid picture
to find the human being
we never stop to wonder
till a person's gone
we never yearn
to know him
till he's packed
and traveled on

sweet beautiful jesus
on a painted cross
polystyrene body
with a superficial gloss
hey were you
jealous of your father
were you short
when you were fully grown
did you like to walk on water
were you scared
to be alone?

i think perhaps tomorrow
i'll try to make a friend
to really get
to know him
instead of pretend
i'll ask him if his feet hurt
has he burdens to be shared
and if he doesn't walk away
i'll ask him
if he's scared
and if he doesn't walk away
if his eyes don't
turn to stone
i'll ask him
if he's scared
to be alone.

i ain't his child

my daddy says
i ain't his child
ain't that something
ain't that wild
daddy says
i ain't his child
ain't that something
wild

my hair is curly
my freckles are tan
could my daddy be
the garbage man
my legs are stumpy
my fingers are short
like my uncle will
who is the
bowling sport
my eyes are slanty
like mister woo
hey
mister laundryman
is it you
i'm ugly as steve
with the big mustache
but mama says poles
are a piece of trash

my daddy says
i ain't his child
ain't that something
ain't that wild

hey
anybody i might

have missed
would you care to state
that i exist
i ain't quite sure
what it is
i did
to make him swear
that i ain't
his kid
but he told mama
and she told me
back when i was
just about three
she felt my face
and she
kind of smiled
and she said
he says
you ain't his child

my daddy says
i ain't his child
ain't that something
ain't that wild
daddy says
i ain't his child
ain't that
something
wild

esther's first communion

when she made her first communion
esther made the perfect union
in her dress of white and wispy veil
esther's parents said to please us
you got to go and marry jesus
and her father took her to the altar rail

when she made her first communion
esther made the perfect union
and that night she thought of him in bed
she decided if he sees us
we ought to get a look at jesus
and she began to see the one she wed

i began to see little jesus
he was sitting on my bed
that's what esther told her mother
and to which her mother said
you're an evil child to tease us
glory be i hope to jesus
that your father never hears this
he would wash your mouth with soap

when she made her first communion
esther made the perfect union
but she never saw his face again
yeah her mother said don't tease us
so instead of seeing jesus
she began to see a lot of other men

what she saw was quite a collection
older men and young ones too
cousins friends and even a brother
one at a time or quite a few
she began to see a gay uncle

who resembled billy graham
she began to see perfect strangers
she didn't even know by name

when she made her first communion
esther made the perfect union
but she never saw his face again
yeah her mother said don't tease us
so instead of seeing jesus
she began to see a lot of other men
but she never told her mother again
no she never told her mother again.

he lives alone

he lives alone
in his great big house
with collages on the walls
and cathedral halls

and he eats at a table
with room for eight
and each course is served
on a separate plate
and he sits by his pool
and he waters his plants
and he does not dance
he does not dance

he lives alone
in his great big house
with his jacobean chairs
and his marble stairs

and he sleeps in a room
with a dozen locks
and his money is kept
in a cardboard box
underneath his bed
(with his mother's ring)
and he will not sing
he will not sing

nothing burns
in the fireplace
leather bound
are the books
a silent film star
lived there once
and a lady comes in
and cooks
and looks after him
(because he pays her well)

he lives alone
in his great big house
and when his pulse
begins to pound
at an
alien sound

he calls in a voice
that can't be heard
to a room down the hall
where no woman stirred
and he thinks of her
and he wishes her there
and he cannot share
he cannot share
oh no he cannot share.

with my daddy in the attic

ba ba ba ba
with my
daddy in the attic
that is where
my being wants to bed

with the mattress ticking showing
and the tattered pillow slip
and the pine
unpainted rafters overhead

with the
door closed on my mama
and my sibling competition
and my shirley temple doll
that truly cries
and my essay on religion
with the pasted paper star
proving tangibly
i'd won the second prize

with my
daddy in the attic
that is where
my dark attraction lies

with his
madness on the nightstand
placed beside
his loaded gun
in the terrifying nearness
of his eyes

with no
window spying neighbors

and no
husbands in the future
to intrude

upon our attic
past the stair
where we'll live on
peanut butter
spread across assorted crackers
and he'll play
his clarinet
when i despair

the veterans big parade

in the veterans big parade
marched the businessmen's brigade
while behind the high school band
the ladies fife and drum corps played
in the veterans big parade
the flag flew high and free

down they marched to fourth and main
our soldiers died but not in vain
god was with us
that's for sure
he proved it cause
it didn't rain
balloons batons you wanted to cry
the best day in july

at the veterans cemetery
then the services were said
there the mayor's first assistant

wiped his glasses
put them on
and read
we're gathered here
dear friends today
to show our brave boys
where they lay
we are with them all the way
and i think it's safe to say
they are not
alone

all the widows proudly smiled
(except for one with an infant child)
picnic time was then announced
and all the little kids went wild
picnic blankets then were spread
and the beer flowed fast and free

there were clams and corn on the cob
to feed the celebrating mob
(once in a while
i don't know why
the infant child
began to sob)
other than that it was new year's eve
till it was time to leave

then a fine hawaiian band
played and sang
aloha oh
and their voices drifted low
between the crosses
painted white
row on row on row
aloha oh
and so goodbye
till next year boys

next july
we are with you
all the way
and i think
it's safe to say
you are not
alone.

michael michael

michael michael
superman
muscle-bound
and supertan
leather jacket
denim pants
never did learn
how to dance
how to dance
digs karate
raps on zen
michael makes it
best with men
digs karate
raps on zen
michael makes it
best with men

michael michael
superman
muscle-bound
and supertan
when he walks
and talks

and moves
michael proves
and proves
and proves
michael is a
hyper superman

pushes acid
peddles hash
that's how michael
gets his stash
rides his cycle
like a king
knows his number
does his thing
does his thing
and if he wants to
he can con
any bird
he's turning on
if he wants to
he can con
any bird
he's turning on

michael michael
superman
muscle-bound
and supertan
when he walks
and talks
and moves
michael proves
and proves
and proves
michael is a
hyper superman

but
late at night
he sometimes seems
to hear
his mother's voice
in dreams
calling to him
clear and plain
but she calls him
mary jane
mary jane
and michael answers
plain and clear
i am coming
mother dear
michael answers
plain and clear
i am coming
mother dear

michael michael
superman
muscle-bound
and supertan
when he walks
and talks
and moves
michael proves
and proves
and proves
michael is a
hyper superman
a superman

beware of young girls

beware
of young girls
who come to the door
wistful and pale
of twenty and four
delivering daisies
with delicate hands

beware
of young girls
too often they crave
to cry
at a wedding
and dance
on a grave

she was my friend
she was invited to my house
and though she knew
my love was true
and
no ordinary thing
she admired
my wedding ring
she admired my wedding ring

she was my friend
she sent us little silver gifts
oh what a rare
and happy pair
she
inevitably said
as she glanced
at my unmade bed

she admired
my unmade bed

she was my friend
i thought her motives were sincere
ah but this lass
it came to pass
had
a dark and different plan
she admired
my own sweet man
she admired
my own sweet man

we were friends
and she just took him from my life
so young and vain
she brought me pain
but
i'm wise enough to say
she will leave him
one thoughtless day
she'll just leave him
and go away

beware
of young girls
who come to the door
wistful and pale
of twenty and four
delivering daisies
with delicate hands

beware
of young girls
too often they crave
to cry
at a wedding

and dance
on a grave

beware of young girls
beware of young girls
beware

twenty-mile zone

i was riding in my car
screaming at the night
screaming at the dark
screaming at fright
i wasn't doing nothing
just driving about
screaming at the dark
letting it out
that's all i was doing
just
letting it out

well along comes a motorcycle
very much to my surprise
i said officer was i speeding
i couldn't see his eyes
he said no you weren't speeding
and he felt where his gun was hung
he said lady you were screaming
at the top of your lung
and you were
doing it alone
you were doing it alone
you were screaming in your car

in a twenty-mile zone
you were doing it alone
you were doing it alone
you were screaming

i said i'll just roll up my windows
don't want to disturb the peace
i'm just a creature
who is looking
for a little release
i said
and what's so wrong with screaming
don't you do it at your games
when the quarterback
breaks an elbow
when the boxer beats and maims
but you were
doing it alone
you were doing it alone
you were screaming in your car
in a twenty-mile zone
you were doing it alone
you were doing it alone
you were screaming

i said animals roar
when they feel like
why can't we do that too
instead of screaming
banzai baby
in the war in the human zoo

he said i got to take you in now
follow me right behind
and let's have no more screaming
like you're out of your mind
so he climbed aboard his cycle
and his red-eyed headlight beamed

and his motor started spinning
and his siren screamed

he was doing it alone
he was doing it alone
he was screaming on his bike
in a twenty-mile zone
i was doing it alone
i was doing it alone
i was screaming in my car
in a twenty-mile zone
we were doing it together
we were doing it together
we were screaming at the dark
in a twenty-mile zone
we were doing it together
alone
in a twenty-mile zone.

mister whisper

when i am going
round the bend
i got a wild
imaginary friend
when i am driven
up the wall
my old friend
he comes to call

mister whisper's
here again
mister whisper's
here again

he's back
in his apartment
in my head
he's back
in his apartment
like i said

just when life
can't get much worse
he tells me
reassuring things
says i'm the
center of the universe
says i'm as good as
presidents and kings

mister whisper's
here again
mister whisper's
here again
i think
i can control him
but instead
mister whisper
takes control
guides my heart
and rides my soul
the minute that
he steps
inside my head

just when i am
sure he'll stay
they shoot me
with a bolt or two
they try to drive
my mister friend
away

and damn it all
they nearly always do

mister whisper
don't go 'way
mister whisper
won't you stay
it gets so lonely
wish
that i were dead
listen whisper
please don't go
listen whisper
don't you know
i'd rather
madness
than this sadness
in my head

the thought
he'll leave
just bitterly burns
and my despondence
grows
as soon as lonely
lonely sanity
returns
and old mister
old mister whisper
goes.

on my way to where

the thought
he'll leave
just bitterly burns
and my despondence
grows
i lost my blue buttons
he sent me
blue buttons
on my birthday
but my blue buttons
came loose
loose
loose
lucy brown
lucy in the sky
luce
lucent
lucid
lucidity
lucifer
light
hang luce
stay loose

i
how did i get this way
i was
what was i going to say
i was on
how did i get here
i was on my
wasn't i here last year
i was on my way

why have they locked me in
i was on my way to
who is my next of kin
christ
won't i ever win
i paid
my airplane fare
i was
on my way to where. . . .

Mythical Kings and Iguanas (1970–71)

mythical kings and iguanas

i have flown
to star-stained heights
on bent and battered wings
in search of
mythical kings
mythical kings
sure that everything of worth
is in the sky and not the earth
and i never learned
to make my way
down
down
down
where the iguanas play

i have ridden
comet tails
in search of magic rings
to conjure
mythical kings
mythical kings
singing scraps of angel-song
high is right and low is wrong
and i never taught
myself to give
down
down
down
where the iguanas live

astral walks i try to take
i sit and throw i ching
aesthetic bards
and tarot cards

are the cords
to which i cling
don't break my strings
(i wish you would)
or i will fall
(i wish i could
i wish i could
i wish i could . . .)

curse the mind
that mounts the clouds
in search of mythical kings
and only
mystical things
mystical things
cry for the soul
that will not face
the body as an equal place
and i never learned
to touch for real
or feel the things
iguanas feel
down
down
down
where they play
teach me
teach me
teach me
reach me.

lemon-haired ladies

whatever you give me
i'll take as it comes
discarding self pity
i'll manage with crumbs
i'll settle for moments
i won't ask for life
i'll not expect labels
like lover or wife
if showing affection
embarrasses you
i will not depend
and i will not pursue
for you are
younger then i
younger than i
younger than i
and i am
wiser than you

the one a.m. phone calls
you're here then you're gone
come when you need me
i won't carry on
i'll simply accept you
the way that you are
unsure and unstructured
my door is ajar
those lemon-haired ladies
of twenty or so
of course you must see them
just don't let me know
don't let me know
whatever you do

for you are
younger than i
younger than i
younger than i
and i am
weaker than you

i'll give you a year
maybe two
maybe three
then what will happen?
where will i be?
you'll still be a boy
but what about me?
what about me?
what about me?

why must you treat me
with such little care
i've so much inside me
i'm aching to share
why am i constant
to someone like you?
children don't know
the meaning of "true"
those lemon-haired ladies
why must you see them?
all that i want in your eyes
is to be them
time is on their side
that's all i lack
i wish you would just
go away
no
come back
come back
go away

come back
go away
what in hell can i do?
i'm supposed to be wise
for i am
older than you
you who are selfish
the games that you play
do as you please
you will anyway
of course you will see them
no use to pretend
for they are
younger than i
younger than i
those lemon-haired ladies
and they will
win in the end. . . .

angels and devils the following day

loved i two men
equally well
though they were diff'rent
as heaven and hell
one was an artist
one drove a truck
one would make love
the other would fuck
each treated me
the way he knew best
one held me lightly

one bruised my breast
and i responded
on two diff'rent levels
like children reacting
to angels and devils
one was a poet
who sang and read verse
one was a peasant
who drank and who cursed
before you decide
who's cruel and who's kind
let me explain
what i felt
in my heart and my mind . . .

the artist was tender
but suffered from guilt
making him sorry
the following day
and he made me feel guilty
the very same way
in his bed on the following day
the other would take me
and feel no remorse
he'd wake with a smile
in the bed where we lay
and he made me smile
in the very same way
in his bed on the following day
the blow to my soul
by fear and taboos
cut deeper far
than a bodily bruise
and the one who was gentle
hurt me much more
than the one who was rough
and made love on the floor.

a stone for bessie smith

isn't it amazing
shakes you to the bone
she bought a stone
for bessie smith
she bought bessie smith
a stone
she got it for
her grave-site
on a temporary loan
but she forgot
she had not paid
for her own
she forgot she had not paid
she forgot she had not paid
after all the contracts
and arrangements had been made
she went to bessie's grave
and marked it with a stone
but she still
had to pay for her own

she went home
to her class reunion
where a classmate
he confessed
she wouldn't want this
getting out
but she used to be the best
in school she was a nice girl
as decent as the rest
though she never was
conservatively dressed

isn't it amazing

you think she could've known
she bought a stone
for bessie smith
she bought bessie smith
a stone
she got it for
her grave-site
on a temporary loan
but she forgot
she had not paid
for her own
she forgot she had not paid
she forgot she had not paid
no sooner had the letters
on the deed begun to fade
when her ashes had been scattered
been battered and been blown
she still had to pay
for her own

she knew
miss gloria swanson
on a tv show they met
they talked across
a hundred years
miss gloria's with us yet
but janis was a gambler
who'd already lost a bet
and the time had come
to settle up
her debt

isn't it amazing
shakes you to the bone
she bought a stone
for bessie smith
she bought bessie smith

a stone
she got it up
for bessie
on a temporary loan
but she forgot
she had not paid
for her own.

the game

i watch the game
aware of tricks
i do not want to see
i do not want to see
a card is palmed
the bets are placed
the loaded dice make three
and no one sees but me
does no one see but me?

the roulette wheel
goes round and round
and stops a bit too short
it's made to stop too short
it's built to stop too short
the chips are down
the croupier laughs
and calls a cheated player sport
he laughs and calls him sport
and the sport laughs with him
the sport laughs with him

there are no clocks
upon the gilded walls
the drapes are drawn

in everlasting night
"we never close"
the neon light
blinks at the sky
"we run an honest house"
the advertisements lie
for i have chanced to glimpse
behind the imitation
antique mirror
and i have seen the pupil
of the boss's
spying eye

pontius pilate's soldiers
gambled at the bottom of the cross
even his ragged robe was lost
so would you kinda care
to tell me boss
what chance have we?
what chance have we?
would you kinda care
to tell me boss?

i watch the game
and if i play
i know i'll go for broke
it must be go for broke
the game is fixed
it's just a
funny
foolish
never ending joke
a never ending joke

the dealer winks
and beckons
with a toothless

taunting grin
i know i cannot win
the game is fixed
okay all right
okay all right
okay all right
god damn it
deal
me
in.

her mother's daughter

see the sweet and genteel lady
so finely boned and frail
see her every morning
at the window with her knitting
where she spends the hours sitting
while she waits
for advertisements in the mail

see the genteel lady
sipping lemonade with lime
once she wanted princes
out of tales that happily ended
now the grocery clerk befriended
her cat and she was
grateful for his time

you'll grow into a beauty
her mother always said
so take your time in choosing
the boy whom you will wed
is this the right one mother?

oh no my daughter dear
there will be someone better
wait another year
is this the best one mother?
the husband that i seek
no he's hardly good enough my child
wait another week
her father died one winter
and was swiftly laid away
oh mother may i marry now?
no i need you will you stay?
i beg you darling daughter
i cannot be alone
if you love me you will stay
if you love me stay at home
damn you mother how i hate you
you will never know how deep
i must cling till you release me
i could kill you in your sleep
i would smile to watch your life blood
flow across your wretched hair
yes of course i love you mother
i will never leave you dear
i swear

see the sweet and genteel lady
she buys beribboned toys
and visits dull relations
to applaud piano pieces
played by nephews and by nieces
she listens in on other people's joys
and looks longingly
at all the passing young boys

yes of course i love you mother
i will never leave you dear
i swear.

yada yada

yada yada yada yada yada
let's stop talking talking talking
wasting precious time
just a lot of empty noise
that isn't worth a dime
words of wonder
words of whether
should we shouldn't we
be together
yada yada yada yada yada yada

let's stop talking talking talking
taking up our lives
saying things that don't make sense
hoping help arrives
curse my questions
damn your qualms
tomorrow they could be
dropping bombs
and we go yada yada yada yada yada

so we sit
at a restaurant table
discussing reasons
we're unable to commit
that's not it
all i want
is to please and enjoy you
what makes you think
i'll be out to destroy you
if you commit
that's not it
is it something you sense
underneath my defenses

that makes me a threat
that's not it
and yet
suppose that's it
ow wow wow i don't want to
think about that now

let's stop talking talking talking
every lame excuse
justifying alibiing
listen what's the use
the sparrow chirps
the chipmunk chatters
and we go on as mad as a hatter
and nothing at all gets said
talk to me please
in bed
where it matters
yada yada yada yada yada.

the lady with the braid

would you care to stay till sunrise
it's completely your decision
it's just that going home is such a ride
going home is such a ride
going home is such a ride
going home is such a low and lonely ride

would you hang your denim jacket
near the poster by Picasso
do you sleep on the left side or the right?
would you mind if i leave on the light?
would you mind if it isn't too bright?

now i need the window open

so if you happen to get chilly
there's this coverlet my cousin hand-crocheted
do you mind if the edges are frayed?
would you like to unfasten my braid?

shall i make you in the morning
a cup of home made coffee?
i will sweeten it with honey and with cream
when you sleep
do you have dreams?
you can read the early paper
and i can watch you while you shave
oh god the mirror's cracked
when you leave
will you come back?
you don't have to answer that at all
the bathroom door is just across the hall
you'll find an extra towel on the rack
on the paisley patterned papered wall
there's a comb on the shelf
i papered that wall myself
that wall myself . . .

would you care to stay till sunrise
it's completely your decision
it's just the night cuts through me like a knife
would you care to stay awhile
and save my life?
would you care to stay awhile
and save my life?

i don't know what made me say that
i've got this funny sense of humor
you know i could not be downhearted if i tried
it's just that going home is such a ride
going home is such a ride
going home is such a ride
isn't going home a low and lonely ride?

Reflections in a Mud Puddle — Taps Tremors and Time Steps (1971–72)

doppelganger

i seem
to see this stranger
almost everywhere
i do not wish
to frighten you
but you should know
he's there
so that if you're threatened
if evil's ever done
you'll know
it's him who did it
you'll know
that he's the one

his looks
are ordinary
but he does things in the dark
he hides inside the shadows
watching children
in the park
he whispers things
in subways
you'd tremble with alarm
i tell you
he will get to you
he's out
to do you harm

i've seen him
in the headlines
and on the evening news
i saw him
on the sidelines

when stones were thrown
at jews
and marching in montgomery
pretending that he cared
i saw him wink
as though
some old conspiracy were shared
he was in the crowd in dallas
at the close of camelot
i spotted him
on campus when
the students had been shot
in an oriental village
with civilians left to rot
he was hanging out
with soldiers
trading heroin for pot
and he was
smiling
smiling. . . .

last night
i found obscenities
scrawled across my wall
i swear
i can't repeat
the filthy words that i recall
and then
the most immoral
damned insulting thing of all
as i read each line
i noticed
his handwriting
was identical
with
mine.

the new enzyme detergent
demise of ali macgraw

mine was a wednesday death
one afternoon
at approximately three-fifteen
i gave up and died
and nobody cried

mine was a bloodless death
not grim
not gory
more like
ali macgraw's new enzyme
detergent demise in "love story"
neat and tidy
unlike christ's on friday

friends were fooled
by the fact
i still breathed
and i spoke
and i smiled
and i lied
in my handy dandy
imitation life disguise kit
i sent away for it
the styrofoam face
fits so neatly in place
with the pre-recorded voice
of your choice
and it almost sounds real
it's a guaranteed deal
and you don't feel a thing
and you can teach it to sing
and all your friends

are deceived
and nobody grieves

mine was a wednesday death
one afternoon
at approximately three-fifteen
i was quietly
laid to rest
and nobody guessed

a handy disposable heart
marks time in a plastic breast
and so it goes
and nobody knows
i am
non
bio-degradable.

the talkative woman
and the two-star general

some other night
my love
some other night you say
of course you're right
dear general
but before you go away
may i please continue
just a moment more
before you close the door
and goodbye
let's see
where was i
what had i just said

oh yes
i was going on about colors
the different kinds
of red

some reds
are like familiar friends
they spring from the growing earth
they flow with the moon
and tides some reds
are the badges of brides
and birth

please
don't lose patience general
stay just a little while
i'm merely speaking of colors
perhaps i'll make you smile

some reds
are unnatural enemies
they crawl out of open veins
they creep
and slide from gaping wounds
like medals of pride
and pain

some reds are close to purple
oh my darling
what do i mean
please
don't put on your jacket yet
some reds are closer to green

some other night
my love
some other night you say
of course you're right
dear general

you're right to turn away
but you recoiled
is something soiled?
to stain a sensitive soul
such as yours
would never be my goal
but i digress
where was i

oh yes
back to the subject of colors
perhaps
if someone tried to wear the reds
of birth and brides
if one could lose his pride
and see the other side
perhaps
he'd have less need
to spill the rude
the cruel
the crawling
reds that kill

you'd better put on
your jacket now
there's beginning to be a chill
such a silly
talkative woman am i
forgive me if you will
for keeping you dear general
sir
you have a quota to fill
while i carry on
about colors
purple green and red
the badges of the living
the medals of the dead.

the altruist and the needy case

he has passion
for ecology
compassion
for minorities
he carries printed placards
to put an end to war
he's a hero
he's a rebel
with a half a hundred causes
he peddles his petitions
door to door

he's at home among the homeless
singing set my people free
he will march
with total strangers
but he will not walk
with me

he writes letters
to his congressman
on indian indignities
black men
are his brothers
he bears collective guilt
he's a prophet
he's a pacifist
but tho' peace
is his objective
he has no fear to see
his own blood spilt

his roots are with the rootless
that's where he needs to be

he will die
with total strangers
but he will not live
with me

he feeds and shelters animals
unselfish are his deeds
he gives away his wordly goods
and has no notion of
my needs
lover look away a moment
tho' the ghetto cries
long enough
to see the hunger in
one person's eyes

passion
for ecology
compassion
for minorities
he weeps to think that anyone
could ever be
alone
he's a seeker
he's a savior
who strives to
save the children
but he's never had
a child of his own

he's united
with the universe
he's at one
with stars and sea
he can love
the whole damned human race
oh

then why is he
so afraid to be
in love
with me?

play it again sam

play it sam
play it again
take me back
to you know when
let's hear it sam
for good old
world war two

play it sam
play it again
gee
the world was
simple then
back when
hearts were brave
and love was true

then
we knew the good guys
then
we knew the bad
right was right
and wrong was wrong
accordin' to mom and dad
(and we believed them)
then a war

was called
a war
proud as trumpet horns
but a rose
by any other name
still has thorns

play it sam
play it for me
take me where
i want to be
back with you
and good old
world war two
far away
i just can't make
today
far as i can be
from good old
world war three
play it uncle sam
for me.

the earthquake in los angeles
(february 1971)

the telephone rang
my sister calling
i got to run i said
nonononono
i just want
to tell you
to tell you

dad is dead
dad is dead?
well when did it happen?
six a.m.
said she
new york time
or california?
new york time
i see

the telephone rang
the week of the earthquake
death was still in the air
at six o one
the walls came down
they never had a prayer
dad is dead?
well how is mother?
good as she
can be
say i said
when dad was goin'
did he happen
to ask
for me?

'member the way
i used to time step
lord it made him proud
he told his friends
(he never told me)
that i stood above the crowd
'member the way
he played the jew's harp
till he broke a tooth
why'd he have
to turn against me

he loved me
once
in his youth

but jesus
i couldn't live his life
make his fantasies real
i couldn't be him
i had to be me
i couldn't make up
for the deal
the dirty deal
he got in this world
he got in
a treacherous world
where six a.m.
suddenly breaks
with senseless death
and shocking quakes
senseless death
and shocking quakes. . . .

the final flight of the hindenburg
(may, 1937)

it's the safest way
i promise you
it's the only way to fly
my daddy said as he pointed up
at the great grey thing
in the sky
the great grey thing
in the sky

pal he said
(he called me pal)
we'll ride in that big balloon
some day we'll fly to londontown
we'll soar like
the silv'ry moon
we'll go to spain
and portugal
we'll fly to paris france
didya know that ship
has a ballroom hall
where it's big enough
to dine and dance
with colored lights
and saxophones
oh yes dad
tell me yesyesyes
and didya know
every night for dinner pal
the people have to wear
full dress?

wah wah wah
wah wah wah
wah wah wah
wah wah

i loved to hear him
talking talking
the safest way to fly
my daddy promised
and i trusted him
despite his
terrible eye
despite his
terrible eye
for i had not yet

felt his wrath
when i gazed at the grey balloon
and i dreamed of
going off with him
by the light of
the silv'ry moon

we ran inside the house
to hear on the
big brown radio
the actual real live
landing broadcast
the big ship was coming in slow
ladies and gentlemen
here she comes
the announcer gaily exclaims
she's gliding in like
a great grey bird
oh god
it's burst into flames. . . .

i dance and dance
and smile and smile
("after an initial deep split
the tremors can go on
indefinitely"; L.A. Times

i'm always loving someone
more than he loves me
lord
i wish
just this once
that's not how it would be

i always try too hard
when i find someone new
god
i wish
just this once
you'd need me more
than i need you

i danced
to please my father
just to win one glance
some sign of his approval
i danced and danced
and danced and danced
i smiled
to make my mother
proud i was her child
to gain some small attention
i smiled and smiled
and smiled and smiled
my books and bikes
i bartered to try
to buy a friend
now i'm grown
this heart i own
is the currency
i spend and spend
and spend
and

in the end
i'll give you
everything i own
sure
you'd never want me
for myself alone
how i hate the way i am

always trying to impress
lord
if i could love me more
i could love you less

and if i could
love you less
i would not
confuse you
dancing
dancing
smiling
smiling
till
of course
i love you. . . .

the aircrash in new jersey

. . . my god
it's burst into flames
i can hear the
screaming screaming
everyone's doomed to
die
sweet jesus folks
it's a terrible sight
the announcer
starts to cry and i look
at my father's
eye
and
it suddenly seemed
too fearful

rimmed-red
as the edge of hell
and it fixed itself
upon me
and it burned
into every cell
it burned
into every cell

oh dad
the broken promises
hurt
more than broken bones
the people's screams
in the ballroom hall
drowned out
the saxophones

wah wah wah
wah wah wah
wah wah wah
wah wah

a great grey frog
now crouches
on the throne
of a former prince
and it's endless
croaking croaking
has no power to convince
oh dad
you did me in that day
with the turn
of your terrible
eye
and
i cannot fly
and i will not fly

and i'm afraid to fly
ever since

wah wah
wah wah
wah wah
wah wah. . . .

aftershock

. . . telephone rang
my sister calling
i'll go on
fighting
his ghost
don't you know dad
the kid that hates
is
the kid that loves
the most
dad is dead?
when did it happen?
six a.m.
said she
new york time
or california?
did he
ask
for me?

what did you say?
never mind
he died in his sleep

god is kind.

Mary C. Brown and the Hollywood Sign
(1972–73)

the hollywood sign

you know
the hollywood sign
that stands
in the hollywood hills?
i don't think
the christ of the andes
ever blessed
so many ills

the hollywood sign
seems to smile
like it's
constantly saying cheese
i doubt if
the statue of liberty
ever welcomed
more refugees

give me your poor
your tired your pimps
your carhops
your cowboys
your midgets
your chimps
give me your freaks
give me your flunkies
your starlets
your whores
give me your junkies

mary cecilia brown
rode to town
on a malibu bus
she climbed to the top

of the hollywood sign
and with the
smallest possible fuss
she jumped off the letter h
'cause she did not
become a star
she died in less
than a minute and a half
she looked a bit like
hedy lamarr

sometimes
i have this dream
when the time comes
for me to go
i will hang myself
from the hollywood sign
from the second
or third letter o

when mary cecilia jumped
she finally made
the grade
her name was in
the obituary column
of both of the
daily trades

i hope
the hollywood sign
cries for the town
it touches
the lady of lourdes
in her grotto
saw fewer cripples
and crutches

give me your poor

your maladjusted
your sick and your beat
your sad
and your busted
give me your has-beens
give me your twisted
your loners
your losers
give me your black-listed

you know
the hollywood sign
witness
to our confusion
a symbol of dreams
turns out to be
a sign of disillusion.

the holy man
on malibu bus number three

when i was two years old
in my mother's arms
on the malibu bus number three
a holy man laid his hand on my head
and said i see i see i see
this here child
she's got two diff'rent eyes
one is dark and one is light
one looks out at the morning
one looks in at the night
some see smiles or some see tears
some see sun or some see rain

but the child who sees both at once
is the child who is destined for pain

i was just two at the time
but i remember it well
when i am lost and lonely
i look for him in religious books
to find his face again
to find his face again
perhaps i will some time
he was hungry and asked for a quarter
he was so hungry
he asked for a quarter
my mother gave him a dime
he blessed her generous contribution
and headed for the door
and he said i got to transfer now
to the bus
the bus number four

i went down to the depot
to look for number four
the station master shook his head
and said four don't run no more
i ride the malibu bus almost everyday
but no one's seen or heard of him
no one's seen or heard of him
(my mother died last may)
he had the nicest smile
just like a silver star
it lit up malibu bus number three
but i don't have two diff'rent eyes
as far as i can see
the right one looks with the body
the left one sees with the soul
was the very last thing
i heard him say

then he took his transfer
and was on his way
he crossed the road to number four
but number four didn't run any more

i don't understand
sometimes i think he was yellow
sometimes i think he was tan
sometimes i think he was a woman
a woman dressed as a man
and though he was old and ancient
and i was less than three
would you laugh
if i should mention
sometimes
i think
he was me?

the midget's lament

there's a prince
inside me crying
howling to be free
raging at my bones
to break apart
in this incompleted frame
there's a hero with my name
there's a unicorn
entangled in my heart

i tell myself i'm sleeping
it's nothing
but a dream
and when i wake

i will not be
the little thing i seem

close your eyes
mary cecilia
close your eyes
and look at me
look at me the way
i'm meant to be
see me with your soul
see me handsome
see me whole
accept my heart
and the unicorn is free. . .

i walk in
i ain't too dumb
i know i got some
handicaps t'overcome
i mean y' seen one midget
y' seen 'em all
oh yeah midget
oh yeah small
and that's as far
as you can see
is that the sum
and the total substance of me?
midgets d-warfs chimps in a zoo
they all look alike to you

well listen good
'cause i don't lie
there's a whole lot more to me
than meets the eye
and it fills my little soul
with midget hate
the way that people won't learn
to differentiate

yeah sure midget
that's what you say
and that's as far as it goes
but have you ever said
that's a hungarian midget?
or that's a midget with
a wart on his nose?

have you ever taken
the time to notice
a midget with curly hair
it isn't fair
there are skinny midgets
fat midgets gay midgets
flat midgets there are midgets
in deep despair

half a soul
half a brain
half a heart
and twice the pain
sure they're cute
and they're a lot of fun
but would you want your sister
to marry one?

midget small
that's it and that's all
the classification's made
midget runt
well now i gotta be blunt
i wish i was born a spade
sure i'd still be a midget
but i would have such
beautiful coloration
and among my fellow midgets
i would be a sensation
talk about

standing out
in the pack
i wish i was black

midgets d-warfs chimpanzees
ain't it all relative
when you're on your knees?
so don't tell me
about minorities
i wish to christ
i wish to christ
i was black.

when a man wants a woman

when a man wants a woman
he says it's a compliment
he says he's only trying
to capture her
to claim her
to tame her
when he wants everything of her
her soul her love
her life forever and more
he says
he's persuading her
he says
he's pursuing her

but when a woman wants a man
he says she's threatening him
he says she's only trying
to trap him
to train him

to chain him
when she wants anything of him
a look a touch
a moment of his time
he says
she's demanding
he swears
she's destroying him

why it it
when a man wants a woman
he's called a hunter
but when a woman wants a man
she's called a predator?

cully surroga
he's almost blind

cully surroga
he's almost blind
one day his eyes just went dim
how could such
a terrible thing occur
when his mother
took such care of him

she cherished him
she nourished him
she praised him to the skies
she polished his mind and his body
so he would be both strong and wise
she saw to it that he had a bicycle
to develop his arms and legs
she read him thoreau and theosophy

she fed him organic eggs
she saw to it he took his vitamin pills
five one-a-days every day
he choked every time he swallowed them
but she never heard
him say one word
but hey mom that's okay okay o
hey mom that's okay okay o
hey mom that's okay okay okay

one day she got this notion
if he stared direct at the sun
he'd get his energy right from the source
it'd shoot through his brain like a gun
and universal light she cried
will penetrate your cells
and it will ring throughout your body
just like metaphysical bells
and you'll be better built
and you'll be better read
and you'll be better able to run
and then in basketball
and in little league
you'll be the graduate number one
mother's son

well he stared at the sun dear mother
he stared every day for an hour
till the sphere began to fade
and the light lost most of its power
and the day went dim
dear god dear mother
and the sweet sun slipped away
and there ain't no sun no more no more
there's just a ball of grey

he wrote that for some reason
whatever

he can't recall
dear mom he wrote
there ain't no sun
he wrote it on a men's room wall
no more sun he wrote
no more shine he wrote
just a ball of grey
other than that mom i'm doin' fine

i take my vitamins five a day
i hang out in bookstores like i should
i meet some well read girls that way
my elimination is very good
so there's nothin' more to say
but hey mom that's okay okay o
hey mom that's okay okay o
hey mom that's okay okay okay.

left hand lost

the left hand is
we always say
the demon devil's side
the left hand does
the dirty work
the shameful things
you hide
judas kissed the left cheek of christ
it's satan's special mark
there were no left-footed animals
allowed on noah's ark
left-handed people are impure
they go against the grain

left-handed children
play with themselves
and drive themselves insane

i was born left-handed
but the nuns
where i went to school
said it wasn't right
and they broke me of it
and now i'm fine
just fine

but sometimes
i get so low so low
sometimes
i get so depressed
as though i lost
a part of me that loved me
the part that knew me best
the child in me that cried
to be cherished
the side of me
that tried to be my friend
the heart of me was living
and loving
but it perished
and i'll never be
completely me again

my right hand fills the china teacups
and needlepoints with old maid aunts
my right hand clings to rosary beads
and waters dying plants
but it's never painted a picture
nor run for president
my left hand
might have done these things
if its roots

had not been bent
a sculptor
a poet
it might have been
instead of a useless thing
to decorate with bangles and bracelets
and my mother's wedding ring

something
it might have accomplished
or nothing
now i'll never know
oh
my lost
my left
my natural hand
my god
i miss you so

the perfect man

i looked up at that perfect man
his long golden hair
his fair and flawless face
his beautiful mustache
he had such grace
he had such grace

i felt his more than perfect arms
so slender yet strong
his fine and faultless hands
the right one wore a silver ring
and gave imperious commands
and gave commands

so sure he seemed
so together and complete
like no man i've ever known
i was dazzled
i was thrown by his strong
persuasive style
and his sweet
self-centered smile

i looked up at that perfect man
and everything came clear
we're not what we appear
perfection is the lie
that covers up the fear
we unsuccessfully try
to hide away

and not once did i cheat
and look down at his feet
knowing they would be grey
and they
would be
made of
clay.

starlet starlet on the screen
who will follow norma jean?

who do you have to fuck
to get into this picture?
who do you have to lay
to make your way?
hooray for hollywood
what do you have to do
to prove your worth?
who do you have to know
to stay on earth?

who do you have to fuck
to become important?
who do you have to trick
to be picked for the flick?
hooray for hollywood
how do you make a virtue of a vice?
who do you have to fuck
to get treated nice?

they lead you
like an animal to slaughter
you're inspected
you're graded
you're stamped
standard or prime
they hang you on a meat hook
where you age
but female meat
does not improve with time
they cut you up
and take the part that's tender
and when they're through
all that's left of you

is tough it's tough
the flesh is willing
but the spirit's growing weaker
enough!
enough!
enough!
enough!
enough!

who do you have to fuck
to get into a movie?
'cause you promised
the home-town crowd
you would make them proud
hooray for hollywood
and you wait for the phone to ring
in a vine street motel
and you write your folks
that being in the movies
is really really swell
well
if that's anyone's idea of heaven
who do you have to fuck
to get to hell?

don't put him down

oh babe
he loves you
but he just can't make it with you
but he just can't tell you it's true
how can he pass the test
when he just can't hardly move himself
let along prove himself the best

oh babe
he wants you
but he just can't get it on as you planned
and i guess a girl just can't understand
how much a guy goes through
all she has to do is let herself
she doesn't have to get herself up
on cue
like a performing seal
in a zoo

how was last night's
performance babe?
was it better than
the night before?
are the old credentials
any good any good any more
or is the act beginning to bore you?

he can sing!
he can dance!
he can juggle!
he's a reg'lar one-man band
his costume's a little tattered
his label says
made in japan

but he beats his battered drum
and he rattles his empty can
and he somehow gets
his flag to fly
looka him
looka him
he's a man!

oh babe
inside him
it's like there's a
little kid in a jail
crying denying he's fragile and frail
hey looka him
he's a male
but it's the wail
of the weary minstrel
it's the dance
of the desperate clown
singing don't put me down
if i fail
please babe
don't put me down
if i fail.

king kong

king kong came to our town
tore our town apart
king kong put the fear of jesus
into every heart

wait says king
wait i said
even though i am dead
wait says king
though i died
hear the other side

king kong came to our town
that's when we employed
decent weapons of defense
and king kong was destroyed . . .

wait says king
you take someone
and put him in a cage
then you shoot him down
'cause he
retaliates with rage

king kong had no feelings
had no christian thought
for the feelings of the folks
he captured and he caught . . .

i captured those
who captured me
i didn't want to die
you say i got no feelings
but you know you lie

once i roamed a handsome thing
in my natural place
here i am repulsive
'cause i'm diff'rent from your race

who decides who's ugly?
who decides who's right?
i tell you
in my jungle
you would be a sorry sight
but we have never caged you
nor put you on display
and when you kill me
with your rifles
don't you know
who it is you slay?

king kong came to our town
tore our town apart
king kong put the fear of jesus
into every heart

fear of god
ain't what you hear
pounding in your ear
christ is dead
i am too
the one you fear is . . .
(king kong came to our town
tore our town apart)
the one you fear is . . .
(king kong put the fear of jesus
into every heart)
the one you fear is . . .
you.

morning star/evening star

when i was a child
you know how children are
i wanted to be
like the morning star
morning is so innocent
trusting and fair
with mother love and angels
reflected on your hair
oh morning star
how warm you are
let me be like you

as i grew up
the morning star
faded into space
then i saw the evening star
standing in its place
i tried to turn away
terrified to find
father love and demons
entangled in my mind
but
despite myself
i saw this other me
oh evening star
how cold you are
it's you
i've come to be

but you see that
once i thought them different
as the moon and sun
but now i know the morning star
and the evening star

are one
mortal immortal
icicle and flame
feminine and masculine
and i am the same

so i hereby
take myself
my soul doth take my heart
to honor love and cherish
till death do us part
i will i will
accept myself
with hope and fear and wonder
and what i have joined together
let no one put asunder.

jesus was a androgyne

jesus was a androgyne
jesus was a he and she
jesus was a freako baby
just like you and me
jesus was a pagan
jesus was a priest
jesus was a beauty
jesus was a beast

anima/animus

give me your poor
your tired your pimps
your carhops your cowboys
your midgets your chimps
give me your freaks
and your hollywood signs
your beasts and your beauties
give me your androgynes

don't you see that
you are all the mother
you are all the son
you're the daughter
you're the father
you are
all in one

you are the least
you are the most
you are the holy
you are the ghost
you're the question
the answer
the even
the odd
you are jesus
you are mary
you
you are
you
are
god

Dory Previn (1974–75)

coldwater canyon

coldwater coldwater canyon
he said he wanted to know her
he had this place in the
canyon
he said he wanted to show
her
coldwater coldwater canyon
he said in a dulcet tone
let's go
to my place in the canyon
where we
can be
alone

well
he had a bed that was
covered
with tiger skin
it was a non-ecological
scene
and she felt so scared
'cause its teeth were
bared
and its smile
was righteously
mean
he had a water
mattress
and a vibrating pillow
designed for decreasing the tension
he had a stereo set
in the headboard yet

and it was featuring
the fifth dimension

high
in a nook on the opposite wall
disguised in a driftwood frame
compatible color tv
tuned to channel three
showing *hunchback of notre dame*
and a huge aquarium
with neon lights
she was quite taken back
by the sharks
and a myna bird
she distinctly heard
making absolutely
rude remarks

coldwater coldwater canyon
he said he wanted to know her
he had this place in the canyon
he said he wanted to show her
coldwater coldwater canyon
he said in a dulcet tone
let's go
to my place in the canyon
where we
can be
alone

well
ain't it great he said
to be all alone?
oh it's a young girl graduate's wish
but then the room went blank
when she looked at the tank
and saw a fish

eat another fish
and the hunchback rang
those notre dame bells
and the bird yelled something risqué
about balloon ascension
while the fifth dimension
rendered up up up up
up up and away

he had
his headphones on
and he was gettin' it off
he had an amy popper in his nose
so he never did see her
leave the room
he never did hear the
screen door close
and she ran ran wild
like a paranoid child
and nothing was aware
of her flight
except the eye
of the sleeping sky
and the ear
of the infinite
still and silent night

coldwater coldwater canyon
poor baby she should have known
coldwater coldwater canyon
you got no grace
if you got no place
to be
alone.

atlantis

i lie in bed
beside him
and i know him
outside in
i've learned his body's
line and length
and memorized his grin
i've counted
every crease
at the edges
of his eyes
i know his soul's
complete circumference
i know
his lies

i know
his outer qualities
i know
his inner doubt
as i know the skin
underneath his shirt
i know
what he's about
i lie in bed
beside him
and unravel him
like twine
i know his depths his drives
his drawbacks
as he
knows mine

i heard they found
the lost atlantis
off the spanish coast
with a host
of hidden secrets
buried signs and symbols
green and guarded gold
and ghosts

i listen
to his breathing
and familiar
tho' he seems
his sleeping self
has wandered
to the regions of his dreams
while
off the coast of spain
the moorish moonlight beams
and deep
in guarded spanish waters
the green gold
gleams

i lie in bed beside him
and i ask him
will you go?
he says i swear
i'll never leave you
i say
i know. . . .

mama mama comfort me

mama mama comfort me
you're the loving one
daddy bought me
electric trains
cause what he wanted
was a son
he wanted a son
oh mama mama where's the joy
in a birthday gun
daddy taught me
how to shoot
cause what he wanted
was a boy
he wanted a son

oh mama mama
don't be down
lift your grievin' head
and tell me what you said
you got no lovin' left around
but don't you understan'
your daddy man is dead?
and i'm alive
but i can't get through
is there anything to gain
if i get out my electric train?
if i should shoot his gun for you
would that tend to please you
tend to ease your pain?

oh mama
i ain't guilty
you're not to blame
what we did is done

sure we failed
our daddy man
cause what he wanted
was a son
to carry his name
but show you love me
show you care
show me mama
and i swear
i will make it up to you
in everything i do
all but one
i ain't your son

i'll always and forever be
always and forever me
me me mama
comfort me.

brando

of course
i always told myself
you know how women get
i'll bet i could have
handled him
if only we had met
where other women failed him
when other women tried
i alone
could cater to
his passions and
his pride

talk about

deflated egos
that was the woman's thing
christ we only felt complete
at the feet
at the feet
of a king

of course
i'm liberated now
i see life as it is
i call my soul
my very own
and i no longer
covet his
no one else can get you through
i've learned
with some regret
i've outgrown all my heroes
i am cured of kings
and yet

and yet
the other night
by chance i saw him
there on the tv screen
overbearing arrogant
marvelous marvelous
and oh so mean
and that old addiction
gripped me
you know how women get
i'll bet i could have
handled him
if only we had met
oh i'll bet
i could have handled him
if only
we had met.

new rooms

i had a vision once
on the super chief
god sat smiling
in the dining car
and when i meet someone
i long to talk of this
and all the crazy things
that makes us what we are

instead we'll chat
of this and that
of politics
favorite flicks
and california wine
i'm awkward
and i balk
at such inconsequential talk
hey by the way
what's your sign?

new rooms new rooms
i hate new rooms
i never know
what i will find
i ring the bell
thinking what the hell
then i chicken out
and change my mind
and just as i'm
about to leave
the door is opened wide
then with pounding pulse
and sweating palms
i find myself inside

new rooms new rooms
i hate new rooms
i never know
just where to look
i go to a shelf
get hold of myself
and pretend to read
a boring book
as though my life
depends on it
what made me come tonight?
afraid no one will talk to me
afraid someone might

and then we'll chat
of this and that
of politics
favorite flicks
and california wine
i'm awkward
and i balk
at such inconsequential talk
hey by the way
what's your sign?

the other night
another new room
feeling caught
and cramped for space
a hand touched mine
timid and fine
but when i turned
to see his face
too many images interfered
too many people pressed
but someone felt
the same as i
dumb and dispossessed

someone else
is lonely too
at least we know
we're not unique
perhaps some time
in another new room
we'll meet again
and speak
of all the crazy things
that make us what we are
god sat smiling
in the dining car. . . .

the obscene phone call

hello hello
is this the P.E.D.?
well i just got
an obscene call
he threatened my life
with a boy scout knife
and a bad invitation to ball
but officer please
put me at ease
would you repeat what you just said?
there ain't nothin' that you
can begin to do
not until i can prove
i'm dead?

hello oh hi
is this the F.B.I.?
got an obscene call
on the phone
he threatened my life
with a boy scout knife
and i'm scared 'cause i'm all alone
what d'you mean
you're on the scene
you are watching me all the time
you got binoculars trained
on my window pane
just in case i commit
a crime?

hello oh hey
is this the C.I.A.?
well this call came
an hour ago
and the F.B.I.
thinks that i'm a spy
and you say you already know
cause you got a bug
in my navajo rug
and my telephone's tapped
of course
well who permitted this game
oh the orders came
they all came from
a higher source?

hello station to station
united nations?
someone called before
and it was real obscene
would you intervene?
oh you're too busy

ending the war
well treaties and pacts
those are big time acts
ending war takes guts and gall
but did you ever explore
what begins a war?
it begins with
an obscene call!

hello G.O.D.
hello this is me
listen god there's this call
that i got
and i've tried them all
tried the big and small
i called the
whole inoperative lot
i tried the F.B.I.
and the C.I.A.
and the keepers of
the country clean
what do you mean
you're inclined to find
this call of mine obscene?
but we've been traced
we've been spaced
we've been human erased
we've been mugged
we've been bugged
we've been detected
we've been . . .
hello god?
we've been
disconnected!

the crooked christmas star, '73

star of wonder
star of night
star of royal
beauty bright
westward leading
still proceeding
guide us with
thy perfect light

he brought me a star
he carved out of wood
he stole from my own back yard
uneven unpolished
repainted unfinished
unwrapped and without any card
hey
how do you like the star
he says
we're out havin' dinner that night
terrific i tell him
and how is your kid?
my kid? oh he's doin' all right
do you think you'll get married?
i ask in my worst
artificial rehearsed
type of voice
eat your chop suey
he orders
then answers
she waited too late
and i don't have a choice
star of wonder
star of whim

royal beauty
burning dim

he brought me a star
he carved out of wood
to hang on my xmas tree
uneven unpolished
repainted half-finished
i think it's a portrait of me
we
only made it but one time
y'know
she wanted to get knocked up
she worked it out
with her astrology chart
i let go of my hot coffee cup
and his elbow is scalded
(the embroidered heart
on his sleeve pulls apart
at the seam)
astrology chart
astrology chart
i better laugh quick
either that or i'll scream!

star of wonder
star of woe
ragged beauty
burning low
the spirit of christmas
is something like love
it's hope
but it's mainly mirage
and after the season
the hope has been lost
with the tinsel you've tossed
behind the garage

the empress of china
she laughs when i laugh
we've both played this scene before
hey how is your kid?
and i don't have a choice
and once more
and once more
and once more
i stare at my fork
the empress would grab it
and stand up and stab it
in his neck
he lies and he cheats
and he eats from my plate
and hates himself 'cause
he can't pay the check!

still
there's the star
he stole with his hands
and carved with his heart
for the limb
at the top of my tree
it's a portrait of me
ain't it also a portrait of him?
a saint who's been tainted
repainted rejected
a dead resurrected
crooked star
he's low but he's high
but hell so am i
ain't that why i love him
i love him
i love him
i love him
i love him

i love him
i love him
i love him
i love him?

star of wonder
star of doubt
ragged beauty
burning out. . . .

did jesus have a baby sister?

did jesus have a baby sister?
was she bitter?
was she sweet?
did she wind up in a convent?
did she end up on the street?
on the run?
on the stage?
did she dance?
did he have a sister?
a little baby sister?
did jesus have a sister?
did they give her a chance?

did he have a baby sister?
could she speak out
by and large?
or was she told by mother mary
ask your brother he's in charge
he's the chief
he's the whipped cream
on the cake

did he have a sister?
a little baby sister?
did jesus have a sister?
did they give her a break?

her brother's
birth announcement
was pretty big
pretty big
i guess
while she got precious
little notice
in the local press
her mother was the virgin
when she carried him
carried him
therein

if the little girl came later
then
was she conceived in sin?
and in sorrow?
and in suffering?
and in shame?
did jesus have a sister?
what was her name?

if the little girl came later
then
was she conceived in sin?
and in sorrow?
and in suffering?
and in shame?
did jesus have a sister?
what was her name?

did she long to be the savior
saving everyone

she met?
and in private to her mirror
did she whisper
saviorette?
saviorwoman?
saviorperson?
save your breath!
did he have a sister?
a little baby sister?
did jesus have a sister?
was she there at his death?

and did she cry for mary's comfort
as she watched him
on the cross?
and was mary too despairing
ask your brother
he's the boss
he's the chief
he's the man
he's the show
did he have a sister?
a little baby sister?
did jesus have a sister?
doesn't anyone know?

We're Children of Coincidence
and Harpo Marx (1976)

children of coincidence

if i hadn't made a left-hand turn
if you hadn't made a right
if i'd waited just a moment more
if you'd missed the light
if that car had never blown its horn
if that friend had stopped to talk
we'd have never met at all
if i didn't take that walk
i'd have gotten there too early
you'd have gotten there too late
we are children of coincidence
coincidence and fate

crossed connections, lost connections
empty corners, crowded intersections
accidents and incidents
we're children of coincidence and chance
if he hadn't stopped to pick it up
if she hadn't dropped the book
when she took it if she'd noticed him
how come we never look?
if she hadn't been so very white
if he hadn't been so black
would she smile and say hello to him?
would he have turned his back?
if she canceled her appointment
would he break his other date?
we are children of coincidence
coincidence and fate

if the planets were in perfect place
if your sign was on the rise
if my stars were in complete accord

but the sun was in your eyes
you'd have only seen my shadow
as i passed you on the street
and it might have been a hundred years
before our souls would meet again
and we would still be strangers
too early and too late
we are children of coincidence
coincidence and fate.

i wake up slow

in the morning
when i wake up
i've got to take an easy pace
when the bed is unfamiliar
then the ceiling is hard to face
so if i ask you
how i got there
don't be mad
if i don't know
i ain't teasin'
here's the reason
i wake up slow

in the morning
when i wake up
if i act like i'm alone
if i'm awful hard to get to
like a disconnected phone
if i ask you
am i dreaming?

don't be mad
if i don't know
i ain't lyin'
i'm just tryin'
to wake up slow

late last night
you said you love me
well i thought
he's just comin' on
and by tomorrow
he'll have come and gone
gone and left me

here to wake up
in the morning
in an unfamiliar bed
where i'll have to face the ceilings
and forget the things you said
so if you move in my direction
don't be mad if i say no
i ain't teasin'
here's the reason
i wake up slow.

for Joby Baker

woman soul

i love him
he's an artist
but he cannot find himself
with puzzled looks
he ponders books
upon some ancient shelf
he does the best he can
that's why i love that man
but i also love
the woman
in his soul

i love him
'cause he questions
all the roles he's forced to play
grown men don't cry
he sees the lie
and cannot change his way
oh but he does the best he can
that's why i love that man
but i also love
the woman
in his soul

joseph oh joseph
i love you
when you're hard
but you know i love you
when you're soft
so why do you discard
the one inside of you. . .?

his heart is torn in two
and he knows he's incomplete
and he won't be whole
until he also
loves the woman
in his soul
woman soul
woman soul
woman soul.

the comedian

his image was impeccable
with every hair in place
discreetly dressed
in a suit and vest
and a cruel, conceited face
he bragged of poor beginnings
and how rich the kid had grown
and he always spoke
to the common folk
like a king upon a throne
he told how far he'd traveled
while the ego trip unraveled
and unraveled for the people to adore
the jokes were lauded
and the audience applauded
more more more more!

with just a touch of modesty
he bowed his gorgeous head
and on his sleeve
did his eyes perceive

an offensive piece of thread?
he tried to pull that piece of thread
he cursed it through his teeth
till he fin'lly found
it was tied and bound
to something way underneath
he told how far he'd traveled
while the piece of thread unraveled
and unraveled till his pants fell to the floor
and the joke was lauded
and the audience applauded
more more more more!

his shirt and tie and underwear
unraveled and untwined
he tried to grin
but now his skin
was beginning to unwind
he tried to make another joke
he tried to grab a prop
while bits of bones
like bits of stones
were getting set to drop
he told how far he'd traveled
while his conscious mind unraveled
and his brain exploded with an awful roar
and the joke was lauded
and the audience applauded
more more more more!

an empty stage
a pile of clothes
the comedian had died
but apart from skits
and comical bits
was there anything down deep inside?
he told how far he'd traveled

but when the person was unraveled
nothing stood where nothing stood before,
and the joke was lauded
and the audience applauded
more more more more!

fours

four
gimme a four
gimme a four
do you hear me?
it takes one quarter
to make one season
it takes four seasons
to make one year
four
gimme a four
gimme a four
do it soon
it takes one quarter
to make one season
it takes four quarters
to make one moon

the four marx brothers
are better than the others
groucho's funny and chico is fine
we know zeppo's only so-so
but harpo wasn't he an androgyne?

four
gimme a four
gimme a four

that'll thrill me
it takes one quarter
to make one season
it takes four quarters
to make one bill
four
gimme a four
gimme a four
gimme a fourth!
it takes four points for
to make one compass
the east and west and
the south and north

the prince is charming?
the dragon is alarming?
the princess phony?
the dwarf is true?
they all hassle
your head is the castle
and all four characters are played by you!

four
gimme a four
gimme a four
fair and square for
it takes four elements
to make one universe
fire water earth and air

four
gimme a four
gimme a four
in the scene
it takes four suits for
to make one deck
an ace a jack a king a queen

hey susito
wouldn't it be neat to
get maria offa her knees?
but see nordeo, he say oh-no!
he say the trinities they come in threes!

four
gimme a four
gimme a four
take me back to
see nordeo
hey susito
mad remia
wholly mackerel!
four
gimme a four
gimme no more
just four see nordeo!
hey susito!
mad remia!
wholly mackerel!

so much trouble

if you weren't
so much trouble
i would take you
back again
'cause the worst
you had to give me
was the best
with other men
now you tell me

your intentions
they are nobler
than before
but you broke
a hundred promises
and you'll break
a hundred more
trouble
you give me trouble
you give me double
the trouble
and triple the trouble
i've got
do i want it?
all that trouble
are you worth it?
no you're not!

if you weren't
so much trouble
i'd be easy
to convince
'cause you took
my body places
where my body
ain't been
taken since
but my heart
had expectations
that you promised
you would fill
but you know
you never even tried
and i know you never will
trouble
you give me trouble
you give me double

the trouble
and triple the trouble
i knew
are you worth it?
all that trouble
do i want to
yes i do!

for Tony Snowdon

taken yesterday

she sat there
at the window
in someone else's dress
bought at an L.A. swapmeet
how was she to guess
he'd want to take her picture
that's what made him stay
just her face
nothing else was
taken yesterday

he hid behind
his camera
he asked her
would she sing
his jeans and his nerve-ends
held in place
with a safety pin and string
she tried
but she was nervous

meeting him that way
just her face
nothing else was
taken yesterday

the africans say
the soul fades away
with every picture
they claim
in five hundred years
when her soul's disappeared
her face will be
the same

with all the endangered species
pelicans poets and whales
she tries to make him
look at her
she tries again
and fails
he left her
but her spirit
will never go
negative grey
just her face
nothing else was
taken yesterday.

the owl and the pussycat

the owl and the pussycat
went to sea
in a beautiful pea-green boat
they took some honey
and plenty of money
wrapped in a five-pound note
the owl looked up at the stars above
and sang to a small guitar
oh lovely pussy oh pussy my love
what a beautiful pussy you are you are
what a beautiful pussy you are

the puss said owl
your mouth is fowl
you birds are unbearable creatures
you get into my bed
instead of my head
and sex is the least of my features

i'm through letting all of you
walk on me
i'm a creature who longs to speak
so take your moon
and your runcible spoon
and shove them up your beak
the owl looked up and said you're right
i'm a cad i'm a creep i'm a cur
and it's a treat to find
an intelligent mind
under all that adorable fur that fur
under all that adorable fur

then he and she
talked of poetry

philosophy and face the nation
and when all was said
she took him to bed
to show him her appreciation
the owl looked up
at the stars above
and sang as she read king lear
oh lovely pussy oh pussy my love
what a beautiful pussy my dear my dear
what a beautiful pussy my dear.

how'm i gonna keep myself together

i lost my job
and i lost my money
well you can laugh
but it wasn't funny
how will i support myself i said
and i held my head
how' i gonna
keep myself together?
how'm i gonna
keep myself together?

a holy man
got up to speak
he said you see
the center's weak
oh well oh well
oh well oh well oh well
ain't that swell!

so i found a job
and it kept me busy

but when i walked
i still felt dizzy
how will i support myself i said
as i fell on my head
how'm i gonna
keep myself together?
how'm i gonna
keep myself together?

a scientist
who rarely spoke
said the albumen
and the yolk
must coexist
underneath the shell
what the hell!

so i bought a cane
and it wasn't too steady
but in my heart
i sure felt ready
now i will support myself i said
as i held up my head
now i'm gonna
keep myself together!
now i'm gonna
keep myself together!

i swore it
to the mountain top
i sang it to the grass
and then i took
one mighty step
and i
fell right on my ass!

so i quit my job
and i spent my money

now i can laugh
'cause now it's funny
now i will support myself i said
'cause I'm out of my head!
now i'm gonna keep myself together!
now i'm gonna keep myself together!

for Robert Carrington

wild roses
(love song to the monster)

the restaurant is crowded
and she hates it when he's late
but she lies when he arrives
she didn't mind the wait
they order soup and meat and wine
she's sane and he's polite
but is there something burning here?
is everything all right?
and whatever happened
to roses to roses red and wild
the kind that grew
in her grandmother's arbor
when she was a child
when the monster smiled?

he spills red wine across the cloth
she tries to let it pass
but she knows
there's something burning here
and shatters with the glass

the monster must be recognized
she hears her body shout
if we don't give it dignity
this plant is going out
and whatever happened
to roses to roses red and wild
the kind that grew
in her grandmother's arbor
when she was a child
when the monster smiled?

we mustn't leave that precious beast
to contemplate its death
to lick its wounds in secrecy
she pauses for a breath
and the smell of something burning here
in the overcrowded room
has disappeared and in its place
is the fragrance of perfume
roses and roses essence of roses
roses red roses wild
the kind that grew
in her grandmother's arbor
when she was a child
and the monster smiled
roses red roses wild roses grateful
the monster smiled.